MARY READ

Library Editions (cloth)

COLONEL WOTHERSPOON and other Plays
Containing Colonel Wotherspoon—What it is
to be Young—The Girl who did not want to
go to Kuala Lumpur—St. Eloi and the Bear.

A SLEEPING CLERGYMAN and other Plays
Containing The Amazed Evangelist—Jonah
and the Whale—Tobias and the Angel—The
Anatomist.

THE SWITCHBACK
The Pardoner's Tale—The Sunlight Sonata.

Separate Editions (wrappers)

MARRIAGE IS NO JOKE
A SLEEPING CLERGYMAN
JONAH AND THE WHALE
TOBIAS AND THE ANGEL
THE SWITCHBACK
THE ANATOMIST
COLONEL WOTHERSPOON

MARY READ

A Play
in Three Acts

by
JAMES BRIDIE
and
CLAUD GURNEY

CONSTABLE & CO LTD
LONDON

First published 1935

PUBLISHED BY
Constable and Company Ltd.
LONDON

.

Oxford University Press
BOMBAY CALCUTTA MADRAS

.

The Macmillan Company
of Canada, Limited
TORONTO

*Enquiries regarding this play should be addressed
to the author's agent, Messrs. Curtis Brown, Ltd.,
of 6 Henrietta Street, London, W.C.2.*

*Copyright 1935 by Osborne Henry Mavor and
Claud Gurney.*

Printed in Great Britain by R. Clay & Sons, Ltd., Bungay, Suffolk

The Play was presented by George Grossmith at His Majesty's Theatre, London, on November 21, 1934, with the following cast:

MRS. READ	Iris Hoey
MRS. AMBER	Isabel Thornton
MARY READ	Flora Robson
OLD MRS. READ	Beatrice Wilson
CAPTAIN SPANNER	Claude Allister
EDWARD EARLE	Robert Donat
A SERVING MAID	Pauline Vilda
A SERGEANT	Arthur Hambling
A ONE-LEGGED SAILOR	Ben Soutten
A RECRUITING OFFICER	Cyril Gardiner
A BARMAID	Eileen O'Mahony
CAPTAIN TAPPIT	Evan Thomas
OCKLES	Ernest Hare
SNYDE	George Benson
SERGEANT CASEY	William G. Fay
A LIFEGUARDSMAN	Edward Wheatleigh
A SLUT	Marie Dainton
ANOTHER SLUT	Millie Sim
ANABAPTIST	Craighall Sherry
SPENLOVE	Paul Chalfont
MRS. RICHARDS	Gertrude Musgrove
CAPTAIN WOODES-ROGERS	John Turnbull
JOHN TRUMPET	Arthur Seaton
A SAILOR	Alex. McCrindle
ANOTHER SAILOR	John Rae
A SHIP MASTER	James Woodburn
DICK CORNER	Charles Farrell
NOAH HARWOOD	Norman Claridge
JACK DAVIS	Charles Morgan
CAPTAIN RACKHAM	Wilfrid Walter
ANN BONNY	Betty Hardy
FEATHERSTONE	Ernest Hare
A CHAPLAIN	Arnold Lucy
A WARDRESS	Gipsy Ellis

The Play was produced by Tyrone Guthrie.

[v]

SCENES

ACT I

Scene   I.   A lodging in Bath, 1712.

Scene II.   Old Mrs. Read's boudoir.

Scene III.   An ordinary in Dover.

ACT II

Scene   I.   A farmhouse in Flanders, 1714.

Scene II.   A dive in Cheapside, 1716.

ACT III

Scene   I.   Governor's House at Providence, Bahamas, 1720.

Scene II.   The after cabin of the *Mallard*.

Scene III.   The deck of the *Mallard*.

Scene IV.   The same as Scene iii.

Scene V.   The prison lazaret at Port Royal, in Jamaica, 1721.

ACT I

SCENE I

SCENE.—*A lodging in Bath in* 1712.

> MRS. READ *is discovered. She is a handsome little round woman of about thirty-eight, with a roving eye. She is quietly dressed.*
>
> *She is washing dishes, etc. To her a heavily-built slut of about fifty carrying a heap of clothes.*

MRS. READ. Oh, it's you, Mrs. Amber.

MRS. AMBER. Yes, Madam. And there, Madam, are the clothes.

MRS. READ. Oh, thank you, Madam. Is your clock correct ?

MRS. AMBER. Everything in my house is the pink of correctness. And the clothes, I hope, are to your liking ?

MRS. READ. Oh, yes . . . yes. I am obliged to you, Madam. (*Takes the clothes and examines them in an absent fashion.*)

MRS. AMBER. I was at some pains to get them for you, Madam. And now perhaps you will kindly . . .

MRS. READ. What in Heaven's name has come to her ? I told her she might walk in the crescent for a few moments. . . .

MRS. AMBER. Yes, Ma'am, a very agreeable walk for a young lady. . . .

MRS. READ. And she has been gone an hour. And it is three o'clock. And her grandmother may be here at any moment. And we are not prepared.

MRS. AMBER. The fashions are very absorbing to a young girl, Madam, and she may well have . . .

MRS. READ. Fashions ! What would a great, lollop-

B

ing lump like that do with the fashions ? Something has befallen her. We are lost.

MRS. AMBER.   To lose a daughter in Bath may well be to a mother's advantage.

MRS. READ.   Mrs. Amber, you will drive me mad. You've seen her ? A pretty young woman of fashion ! Look at me, would you have thought that a woman of my figure would give birth to a daughter like a plough-boy ?

MRS. AMBER.   She is a bold, manly sort of wench, but . . .

MRS. READ.   And you talk to me of the fashions. She has stopped to look at a dog-fight.

MRS. AMBER.   I shall send one of my girls to look for her.

MRS. READ.   Do, Madam, quickly. It is a matter of life and death.

MRS. AMBER (*changing her tone perceptibly*).   Indeed, Madam, it would seem so. (*She has checked herself on the way to the door.*)

MRS. READ (*at the window again*).   Thoughtless slut ! I have the planning and the working while she sulks and dreams. Why, we should have walked from Exeter, every hard step of the way, but for a smile to the carrier. And who smiled at the carrier ? I did. And not a word from Mistress Sullen, good or bad, for all the ride.

MRS. AMBER.   One moment, Madam. Did my ears deceive me or did I hear you say that you would have walked . . . walked . . . from Exeter ?

MRS. READ.   Every hard step. And where is she now ? She knows as well as I do that everything may miscarry if she fails to play her part. And she is late—late—late when a few minutes may make all the difference between affluence and penury. And one would imagine that after all these years of pinching and scraping and begging a crust from the neighbours . . .

MRS. AMBER.   Madam. . . . Lookee, Mrs. Read, or whatever you call yourself, I have a word to say to you.

[2]

MRS. READ. What is it, Mrs. Amber? I am sorely discomposed.

MRS. AMBER. And so am I, Madam. The price of that suit of clothes is three guineas, and I shall be obliged by your lodging money in advance.

MRS. READ. One would have thought . . . What did you say?

MRS. AMBER. You heard very well what I said, Madam.

MRS. READ. But, Mrs. Amber! You shall be paid.

MRS. AMBER. I know that, Madam.

MRS. READ. I cannot sufficiently thank you for what you have done and . . .

MRS. AMBER. Yes, you can. Quite sufficiently. And I intend that you shall. Zounds, here's a pretty business. There was no talk of crusts and tramping like Romany tinkers on the Exeter road when you sailed into my fine lodging like the Duchess of Marlborough paying a visit to the Queen's majesty. You pay for these clothes or you find yourself in the stocks, and that sharply.

MRS. READ. You cannot intend that, Madam.

MRS. AMBER. I can't can't I? You canting, cheating baggage!

MRS. READ. Mrs. Amber! . . . Mrs. Amber, I will be frank with you. I am a widow. . . .

MRS. AMBER. *That* is not, in itself, a recommendation. Do you suppose I should have trudged the town to get these slops if I had known the sort you were?

MRS. READ. But you shall be paid. Every penny. The visitors I am expecting . . .

MRS. AMBER. Visitors! What visitors? Where are they? Do you think you can cozen an old warrior like me with a monkey trick like that? Get out into the street. You have been here too long already. My other guests will be scratching. (*She advances menacingly.*)

MRS. READ. Keep back from me.

MRS. AMBER. Will you pay? (*Grasps* MRS. READ'S *right hand in her left.*)

[3]

MRS. READ.   I shall faint.   I am a lady.   I am a gentleman's widow. . . . Oh!

[MRS. AMBER *grips her roughly by the arm and shakes her between each word.*]

MRS. AMBER.   Have . . . you . . . any . . . money?
MRS. READ.   Help!   Help!   Help!   Mary!   Mary!

[*Feet are heard running and a tall ungainly girl bursts into the room.*   MRS. AMBER *turns to face her.*]

MARY.   What's the matter, Mother?
MRS. READ.   Oh, thank God you've come.
MARY.   What's the matter, Mother?   What is it?
MRS. READ.   She caught me by the arm.   See.   It's black and blue.
MARY.   I can't see anything the matter with it, Mother.
MRS. READ.   She says she will have us thrown into the street.   (*Begins to cry again.*)
MARY.   Don't cry, Mother.   She shan't harm you.
MRS. AMBER.   Look you here, Mistress . . .
MARY.   Stand back, Madam, please.
MRS. AMBER.   Oh, I'm to stand back am I?
MARY.   Yes, if you please.   Mother, what does she want?   Don't cry, Mother, tell me, what does she want?
MRS. AMBER.   I want my fair due.   Have you got it?
MARY.   Have you explained to her, Mother?
MRS. AMBER.   I want no explanations.   I want three guineas for this fine suit of clothes *and* my lodging money in advance.
MARY.   But that isn't usual.
MRS. AMBER.   Nor it isn't usual for a pack of Romany tinkers and carriers' roadside trulls to come peacocking into my lodging like gentry.
MRS. READ.   I've never been spoken to like that before.
MRS. AMBER.   Haven't you?
MARY.   Yes, we have.   Too often.   It isn't a crime to be poor.

[4]

MRS. AMBER.   It's a crime to try and bilk a decent landlady.   Have you got the money?

MARY.   No, we haven't.

MRS. AMBER.   Then out of here.   Out you go.

MARY.   No. . . . We're not going.

MRS. AMBER.   You're not going, aren't you?   Then it's the stocks for you, my lady. . . . Get away from that door.

MARY.   Stay where you are.   I'm stronger than you are.   I'm as strong as a man.   If you fight with me, I'll break your back.

MRS. AMBER (*hesitant*).   You thieving termagant! (*She rushes to the window.*)   We'll see if decent law-abiding citizens are to be . . .

MARY.   Mrs. Amber!

[*She says the words in a voice that is later to shake the nerves of Captain Rackham's crew.   It checks* MRS. AMBER.]

MRS. READ.   Mary!

MARY.   Tell her not to do that.   Tell her not to do it.

MRS. READ.   Mary, don't look like that.   Mrs. Amber, Madam, come back from the window . . . I beg you, I implore you to let us stay.

MRS. AMBER.   Don't let her near me.   She made my heart stop beating.

MRS. READ.   Don't heed her, Ma'am.   She means you no harm.   Only listen to me.   If you knew, Ma'am, all the circumstances, you wouldn't, you couldn't turn us away.

MRS. AMBER.   Couldn't I?   I wouldn't let you stay if you paid me a thousand pound.

MRS. READ.   But listen, Ma'am.   Pray listen.   It is to your own interest, Ma'am.   You must help us. Mary, tell the lady you're sorry.

MARY.   I did her no harm. . . . Something happened to me.   I am sorry.   Tell her the truth, Mother.   Go on.

MRS. READ.   We are not what we seem to be, Madam.
I am the lawful married wife of William Read of Ipplepen
in Devon, and I have the lines to show it.

MRS. AMBER (*sitting down and striving to recover the
initiative*).   What's all this got to do with me?

MRS. READ.   Pray have patience, Ma'am.   I was
lady's-maid to Mr. Read's mother, Ma'am.   He . . .
I . . . My father made him marry me. . . . It is
painful, Ma'am, as you can well understand. . . .

MARY.   Go on, Mother, go on.

MRS. READ.   Mr. Read's mother was a very hard lady.
A good, *Christian* woman, but hard and cruel.   She
would have nothing to do with me, and I fear that after
our little boy was born I let poor Will—Mr. Read, Ma'am
—hear but long and bitter reproaches.   I blame myself,
Ma'am; I blame myself entirely for what followed.

MRS. AMBER.   What followed, Ma'am?   Come to the
story.

MRS. READ.   It is an old story, Ma'am.   Mr. Read
ran away to sea.   I never saw him again.

MRS. AMBER.   Then this young person here?

MRS. READ (*turning on the ready tear*).   Alas! She . . .
I . . .

MARY.   I am a bastard, Ma'am.   I have no father.

MRS. READ.   Alas, that I should have to confess it to
one of my own sex.

MRS. AMBER.   I thought as much!   And now . . .

MARY.   One moment, please!   We are in desperate
case.   Mrs. Read is grown old.   She has written my
mother to say that she has a longing to see her grandson
before she dies.   My half-brother is dead, but she does not
know that.   It is my mother's intention that *I* should take
his place.

MRS. AMBER.   Take his place?

MRS. READ.   Yes, yes.   That is why we wanted the
clothes.   Mrs. Read is rich.   We shall get money, and
you shall be paid.   Only you must—you must help us.

MRS. AMBER. So that's the way of it, is it?

MARY (*with the same ring in her voice*). That's the way of it.

MRS. AMBER. And if I call a constable? I suppose it would be no novelty to you, Mistress, to be thrown into the street, in the kind of life you have been leading?

MARY. In the kind of life we have been leading I have more than once had to defend my virtue with my fists.

MRS READ. Mary, Mary.

MARY. If you call the whole town guard . . .

MRS. AMBER. You speak boldly, Mistress.

MARY. We won't be baulked at the last minute by the like of you.

MRS. AMBER. You won't, won't you?

MARY. No, we won't. There's no time to lose. . . . Come, take the hazard! Come on!

MRS. AMBER. Rat me, I'll do it. (*Big laugh from all.*) I'll help you to cozen the old trot. Rat me, it's like one o' them bawdy plays. Ods my life, she'll make a fine upstanding bully boy. Come, Ma'am, we'll look to the gear.

[MRS. AMBER *and* MRS. READ *go up to bed.*]

MRS. READ. Oh, Ma'am, a mother's blessing on you. You shall not regret it.

MRS. AMBER. Regret it? Why the devil didn't you tell me all this before? The silver's a thought tarnished, and here's a seam . . .

MRS. READ. Oh, they will serve well enough.

MRS. AMBER. Come, young gentleman, off with your petticoats . . .

MRS. READ. God ha' mercy, not here.

MRS. AMBER. Come with me to my room. Here, I'll take the slops.

[*Takes the clothes from* MRS. READ.]

MRS. READ. And make haste.

[7]

MARY.   I'll make haste.

[MRS. AMBER *and* MARY *exit* R.C.]

MRS. READ *is all hot and bothered for an instant. She then first runs to the table and clears dishes on the table to the top of the cupboard* D.R. *She then flutters to the cupboard* U.L. *and takes out two papers.*

[*Knock.*]

[*She runs to the door calling out " Mrs. Amber, Mrs. Amber! "* MARY *rushes in asking for ribbon.* MRS. READ *shushes her out quickly.*

MRS. READ *then runs and gets a small knee desk from the top of a tallboy* U.L. *and puts it on table. She then gets pen and ink out of cupboard* U.L. *and puts them on table, then places the two papers on top of tallboy. Then lastly she arranges the chair in front of the window* L.

[MRS. AMBER *knocks.*]

MRS. READ *runs to the* R. *for a last look at mirror over the fireplace, then gives a feeble " Come in " from in front of the bed.*]

MRS. AMBER (*comes just inside door*). Your guests, Madam.   Be so good as to come this way, Sir and Madam.

[OLD MRS. READ *and* CAPTAIN SPANNER *enter.* MRS. AMBER *exits, closing door after her.*]

OLD MRS. R. (*just below level of bed-post*). Well, Hannah! . . . Take my comfit-box, Archibald, and give me my handkerchief. (*Throws her stick on bed.*) That staircase has brought me all out in a sweat.   And leave the comfits alone.

SPANNER (D. R.). Fore Gad, Madam, do you take me for a thief?

OLD MRS. R. Why not?   When you've stolen one old woman's heart.

[*Throws him her handkerchief.*]

[8]

SPANNER.   Rot me, that was a fair exchange.

OLD MRS. R. (*crossing stage*).   You are an idiot.

[OLD MRS. R. *finds her way to settee* L.C., *sits*.]

SPANNER (*following but above table*).   You are to blame for that.   A lover in his senses?   What a conception!

OLD MRS. R.   Well, Hannah, so I see you at last.

MRS. READ (L.).   I am deeply sensible of your generosity Madam.   I cannot conceal from myself how painful it must be to behold one who so basely misused the countenance of so kind a benefactor.

OLD MRS. R.   And very prettily spoken too.   Let me see. . . . It must be a good twelve years since . . . Where the devil . . . Give me my handkerchief.   Since my unhappy boy . . .

MRS. READ.   Nineteen years, Madam . . .

OLD MRS. R.   Is it bedamned?   We'll let that pass. You've brought my grandson with you?

SPANNER.   Your grandson?   Ah, Madam, I still believe it a dream.

OLD MRS. R.   Hold your tongue.   Well?

MRS. READ.   He is here, Madam.

OLD MRS. R.   Where?

MRS. READ.   He awaits you in an adjacent chamber. I thought it well, Madam, to be assured that you were willing to receive him.   He is a sensitive lad.

OLD MRS. R.   A milksop is he?   Then he's not my William's boy.

MRS. READ.   Indeed he is, Madam (*up to Cupboard*). I have an extract from the Parish register to prove it.

[*Gets paper and gives it to* SPANNER. *She takes a document from* MRS. READ *and hands it to* SPANNER.]

OLD MRS. R.   Oh, you have, have you?   Read it, Spanner.   What does it say, Spanner?

SPANNER.   Stap me, it reads all right.

[9]

OLD MRS. R.   We can accept it?

SPANNER.   Oh, I think so, Madam.

OLD MRS. R.   Very well, then. I may tell *you*, Hannah, that whatever I may decide to do for the boy you need build no hopes on any favours for yourself. The very sight of you sets me retching. Give me a jujube!

[SPANNER *gives her one.*]

MRS. READ.   I am sorry you should be so discomposed, Madam.

OLD MRS. R.   And I will have no blubbering and clinging, you understand?

MRS. READ.   Yes, Madam.

OLD MRS. R.   And if the lad comes under my protection you take yourself off for good, you understand?

MRS. READ.   Yes, Madam. But you will appreciate that a mother's heart . . .

OLD MRS. R.   Mother's heart be damned! You had little enough thought of mothers' hearts when you seduced my only son.

MRS. READ.   Very true, Madam. And I have suffered for it bitterly. But the thought of your William may awaken an answering chord in your heart when I tell you that my William is very dear to me.

OLD MRS. R.   M'! Yes?

MRS. READ.   And if I am to lose my boy I do not know what I shall do. The space between this day and the silent grave will be dark and gloomy and wet with tears. I need not assure you, Madam. Indeed, had I not been driven by stern necessity . . .

OLD MRS. R.   Ugh! How much do you want?

MRS. READ.   Nothing, as you can perceive, Madam, can allay my sorrow, but I had thought, as a minimum, Madam, of a hundred guineas.

OLD MRS. R.   You may think again, Hannah, and I should recommend you to think in a more prosaic and less grandiose fashion.

SPANNER. A hundred guineas! A fortune, by Pluto.
A hundred guineas for a hawbuck hobbledehoy who . . .

OLD MRS. R. Captain Spanner! That young gentleman is my grandson, with the blood of the Trevennicks
in him through me and be damned to it! and I'll thank you
not to forget it.

SPANNER. My Theodora! Say not that my Theodora is angry with her Lysander.

OLD MRS. R. Quiet! Where is thy urchin, Hannah?
God forbid he take after thy side of the house or you both
go packing.

MRS. READ. I shall fetch him, Madam, at once.

[She curtseys and goes.]

William! William! Willie boy!

SPANNER. My Theodora. I am stricken to the earth.

OLD MRS. R. Zounds, you deserve to be. Who are
you, I should be happy to know? A damned macaroni
bravo that hadn't a shirt but the one he mouched off a
hedge till I picked him out of the gutter.

SPANNER. Have a care, Madam. There are words
a gentleman finds it hard to brook. And the word gutter,
Madam, is one.

OLD MRS. R. If you don't like my way of speaking,
you must go and sponge on someone who speaks prettier.

SPANNER. Sponge, Madam?

OLD MRS. R. That's what I said.

SPANNER. I cannot believe my ears. There is only
one thing left for me to do.

OLD MRS. R. What is that, pray?

SPANNER. I shall go at once to my lodging; write a
heart-rending versicle to an address you may conjecture;
and then, Madam, I shall cut my throat, rot me.

OLD MRS. R. Fiddlesticks!

SPANNER. A sponge! You called me a sponge.
(*In tears.*)

[11]

OLD MRS. R.   Wella, wella! There, there! Wring thyself out, my lamb. . . . Hush!

[*Enter* MRS. READ *leading in* MARY *in boy's clothes. She makes an agreeable diffident youth.*]

MRS. READ (*coughs*). (*Curtseying*). Madam, your grandson. (*A pause.*)

OLD MRS. R.   What's your name, young fellow?

MRS. READ.   Will, Madam, after his poor dea . . .

OLD MRS. R.   Hasn't the boy a tongue? Can't he speak for himself? He doesn't look a half-wit. A well-grown lad. He favours the Reads, thank God. Will you kiss your old Granny?

MARY.   Certainly, if you wish it, Ma'am.

[*She kisses old* MRS. READ, *gravely and without enthusiasm. Then backs to below chair* L.]

OLD MRS. R.   How would you like to live with me and be brought up a gentleman?

MARY.   I should like of all things to be a gentleman, Ma'am.

OLD MRS. R.   And you shall be. Captain Spanner here will teach you.

SPANNER (*sulkily*).   A privilege, Madam, 'fore God.

MARY.   I am obliged.

OLD MRS. R.   So that is settled. I like you. You like me. And now . . .

MARY.   But, Madam . . .

OLD MRS. R.   But what, boy?

MARY.   I cannot leave my mother unprovided.

OLD MRS. R.   I'll provide for your mother all right.

MARY.   We should like that, if you please, in writing.

OLD MRS. R.   In writing?

MARY.   Yes, if you please. On my advice my mother prevailed upon a notary in Exeter to prepare a deed. You have it, Mother?

MRS. READ. Yes, dear. Here it is. (*Gets deed from chest.*) Would the—would you—would the gentleman be pleased to cast his eye over it ?

SPANNER. As you wish.

[SPANNER *sits on bed, draws* MRS. R. *beside him, and they con the document.*]

OLD MRS. R. Sit down ; you are no fool.

MARY. I hope not, Ma'am. If I have taken a liberty, Ma'am . . .

OLD MRS. R. You didn't get your brains from your mother's side.

MARY. Possibly not, Ma'am.

OLD MRS. R. You seem to me to be a very hard, calculating young man.

MARY. I hope not, Ma'am.

OLD MRS. R. You do not seem to me over-endowed with natural feeling.

MARY. I find my situation somewhat strange, Ma'am. That is all.

OLD MRS. R. We shall get on well together, I think. I have a certain hardness myself.

[*Big laugh from* SPANNER *and* MRS. READ.]

[*A gallantry from* CAPTAIN SPANNER *results in an ill-suppressed titter from* MRS. READ. OLD MRS. READ *turns furiously upon them.*]

'Zounds, what's all this ?

MRS. READ. It is nothing, Madam. The Captain said . . .

SPANNER. A piece of harmless waggery, Madam.

OLD MRS. R. This is no occasion for waggishness. What does the writing say ?

SPANNER. There is a forest of whereases and inasmuches, Madam, but the fact does emerge that Mrs. Read will relinquish her son and promise never again to approach his person in consideration of the sum of two hundred guineas.

[13]

OLD MRS. R.   'Sblood! Two hundred? Two. . . .
Look you, Mistress, you said a hundred.

MARY.   Did you, Mother?

MRS. READ.   It may have slipped out.

OLD MRS. R.   A hundred, she said.   And a monstrous
sum at that.

MARY (*rises*).   You do not wish to pay my mother two
hundred guineas?

OLD MRS. R.   I do not, and that's a fact.

MARY.   Then it is a great pity, Ma'am, and we are
very sorry, but we must wish you good-day.   (*Bows.*)

OLD MRS. R.   What did you say, boy?

MARY.   I said we must wish you good-day.

OLD MRS. R.   Who taught you to shove in your beak
when your elders were talking business?

MARY.   Experience, Madam.

OLD MRS. R.   D'you think for one moment that I
shall sign that monstrous sheet?

MARY.   I had hoped you would, Madam. I have
ambitions to be a gentleman.

OLD MRS. R.   Very well, then.   You shall take your
hundred guineas, and . . .

MARY.   Two hundred, Ma'am.

OLD MRS. R.   You set a high value on yourself.

MARY.   Yes, Ma'am.

OLD MRS. R.   My last word is a hundred and fifty pounds.

MARY.   My mother must be provided for.   Two
hundred guineas, Ma'am.

OLD MRS. R.   So be it.   Two hundred pounds.

MARY.   Guineas.

OLD MRS. R.   Give me the pen.

[*Tongue protrusion, hard breathing and signature.*]

Take that.

MARY.   Thank you, Ma'am.

OLD MRS. R.   And of all the obstinate young mules . . .

MARY.   Thank you, Ma'am.

[14]

SPANNER. Stap me, a princely bit of generosity.

OLD MRS. R. Come, Spanner, I owed it to the son of my poor lost boy. (*Rises.*) Spare us your tearful farewells, Hannah.

MARY. I shall follow you, Madam, if I may, within half an hour. I may wait on you at your house?

OLD MRS. R. Yes, Will. But lose no time. (*Just out of door turns.*) Come, Captain Spanner.

> [OLD MRS. READ *and* SPANNER *go. The* CAPTAIN *contrives to throw a rose to* MRS. READ. *After* MARY *shuts door big laugh.*]

MARY. Was that well done, Mother?

MRS. READ. Oh dear, oh dear, oh dear! (*hysterically*).

MARY. Compose yourself, Mother. I did well, didn't I?

MRS. READ. I wish I had your hard, cruel heart, Mary dear. (*Putting deed in reticule.*)

MARY. Do you suppose I wish to go to that foolish, wicked old woman? I greatly prefer you to her. You sing prettily and you have pretty ways, though you will be for ever ogling every man you meet. (*Sits back on heels.*) Mother, who was my father?

MRS. READ. My only failing, my dear, is a plaguy weak memory. Besides, one cannot always tell, for sure.

MARY. I see (*rising*). Oh what a mort of silliness and horror I renounced when I threw off those petticoats for good. What will you do now, Mother?

MRS. READ. Who knows? (*To mirror*). I passed a most genteel mantua-maker's yesterday . . .

MARY. Yes, yes, Mrs. Workadays. That blue velvet would become you very well, Mother, and with a little lace on the . . .

MRS. READ. Lack-a-daisy, here's a brisk young man with his blue mantuas!

MARY. I forgot (*with a laugh*).

MRS. READ. Nay, but this is a serious matter. You might betray yourself in dozens of ways, and then we should be branded and transported.

[15]

MARY (*sitting on table*).   It will be easier than I thought.

MRS. READ.   What will be easier ?

MARY.   To forget that I've been a girl.

MRS. READ.   To forget ?

MARY.   It will be like a long bad dream.

MRS. READ.   Well, I must say that's a nice thing to say to your mother.

MARY.   I can't help it, Mother.   There has been a change.   I didn't think there could be such a change.

MRS. READ.   I am glad you take it in that fashion. Only, don't change again and come running back to my apron-strings.

MARY.   I won't do that.   I'm free now.

MRS. READ.   So am I (*to mirror* R.).   That's what I'm telling you.

MARY.   You ?   Free !

MRS. READ.   Yes.   And I may tell you, my dear, putting aside a mother's natural feelings, I don't think I could be bothered with you again.

[*Looking in mirror all the time.*]

MARY.   I shall never bother you again.   A new way of living is a new life.   No more chattering and whispering and side glances for me.   I'll talk out roundly, looking my fellows in the eyes.   Oh, poor mother, with your talk of freedom and your whalebone and your quilting and your laces and your ribbons and your suffocating smell of musk.   *I have legs and arms now.*   I can swing my arms.   I can walk a full pace.   I can breathe . . . I'm myself at last.   Good-bye, Mother.

MRS. READ.   The Lord restore your sense, my dear.

MARY.   Good-bye. (*Goes out.*)

[MRS. READ *sees* MARY *out of door, runs to window singing with orchestra.*]

MRS. READ (*at window*).   Good-bye.

CURTAIN

ACT I

SCENE II

SCENE.—OLD MRS. READ's *boudoir, a few weeks later.*

OLD MRS. READ *is sitting for her portrait.* EARLE *is painting her. The audience is allowed to observe that his hands are labouring in his own interests and his tongue is in his cheek.* MARY *sits on a table, swinging her legs and punching holes in a surcingle. She looks impatient and sulky.* OLD MRS. READ *is fidgety but in high good-humour.*

OLD MRS. R. May I speak ? May I speak now ?

EARLE. Eh ? Oh, yes.

OLD MRS. R. It won't throw my dimple out of drawing ?

EARLE. Madam, your dimple is already fixed and immortal. At the moment I am doing your stomacher.

OLD MRS. R. Oh, la. Then if I keep my stomach steady I can talk as much as I like ?

EARLE. Within reason, Madam. If that is possible.

OLD MRS. R. You are a tease, Mr. Earle. I wonder, Will, you allow him to treat me so.

MARY. What were you saying, Grandmamma ? I wasn't paying attention.

OLD MRS. R. No. I thought you weren't. He might be making the boldest advances to me, and you—— Did you ever know such a hobbledehoy, Mr. Earle ? Even if he has no interest in a poor old woman, one would think that he would at least try to acquire some graceful accomplishments. And I will say this for painting, it is a graceful accomplishment.

C

[17]

EARLE. It is encouraging to us all that you should think so.

OLD MRS. R. Mr. Earle. Do you think you could spend the rest of the sitting in painting the curtains and the table and whatnot? To tell you the plain truth— (*simper*)—I am expecting a visit from—well, from a gentleman, and I have certain instructions to give my maid.

EARLE. As you wish, Madam. I shall paint the curtains and whatnot with such elegance and devotion that the whole world will grow faint with envy of the possessor of such curtains and whatnot.

OLD MRS. R. You are a sad wag, sir.

EARLE. No, Madam, no. I shall project, Madam, your personality into your surroundings. They shall be haunted curtains. Your moods and graces shall hang in their folds like—like a pipe tobacco smoke. They shall breathe and smell, I swear, not of themselves, though they are very nice indeed, but of thee. Only not to-day, if you will forgive me. And do not let me detain you. I would rather die than do that.

OLD MRS. R. 'Od rot it, what a speech.

EARLE. I am glad you like it, Madam; it was from the heart.

OLD MRS. R. I hope you paint as well as you speak. May I look?

EARLE. Yes, if you wish.

OLD MRS. R. Oh, blast my knee-joints. (*Rises.*) (E. *tries to help her.*) Don't help me, dammit. And they call this a spa. Ods figgins, am I as ugly as that?

EARLE. I have not finished yet, Madam.

OLD MRS. R. It has a look of my chin, but the hands...

EARLE. I shall put them right to-morrow.

OLD MRS. R. I hope you will. When you have finished, hide the thing. I wouldn't for the world my gentleman friend saw it as it is just now.

EARLE. Very well, Madam.

OLD MRS. R. Never stir alive. My legs are like two

tombstones. Oh, what I suffer for vanity. Bury thy traps, be sure, Mr. Earle. I must haste. (*Little laugh.*) Cecily! Cecily!

[*She goes out* R.]
[EARLE *continues painting. Whistles a few bars.*]

EARLE. You are not very curious to see what I've done with your grannie, young fellow.

MARY. No.

EARLE. Why?

MARY. No. It is a lying picture.

EARLE. What do you say?

MARY. You paint lies. It is bad enough to waste your time on a womanish business like painting, when every decent man is at the wars, but you shouldn't paint lies.

EARLE. Well, in all my life!

MARY. Mr. Earle. . . . In some ways you are better than any man I ever saw. It makes me sick to see you playing the flattering liar and the coxcomb and the poltroon.

EARLE. That's the Trinity of success, my dear Sir. A man must be all three these days, or find himself in Queer Street.

MARY. I see no " must " about it.

EARLE. There is a " must " about nearly everything.

MARY. What do you mean by that?

EARLE. I mean that you and I must be cleverer cheats than we look to cheat our destiny.

MARY. Destiny? What is my destiny?

EARLE. Let me look at you. (MARY crosses to C.)

MARY. Can you see the future?

EARLE. God forbid.

MARY. Then how do you know my destiny?

EARLE. I see it in your eyes. (*Pause.*) I see rashness and fear sitting side by side, and something else I don't understand.

MARY. You must know a great many things.

[19]

EARLE. Yes. And none of them of the smallest service to me.

[*A very long pause.*]

MARY. Mr. Earle . . . oh, nothing. You can't help me. We have to help ourselves in this world.

EARLE. That's a heavy load for a youngster to carry. The world doesn't please you very much.

MARY. I think there is something amiss with it, Mr. Earle, but perhaps that is because I haven't learned to use it properly. It seems a fine enough world when I'm learning to fight or to shoot or to ride; or when I'm talking to you about queer peoples and countries, or when I'm dreaming of seeing them. But then again it grows ugly, like . . .

EARLE. Like the turning-point in a nightmare?

MARY. Yes. You seem to know the things I want to say.

EARLE. I think I shall paint your portrait.

MARY. No.

EARLE. Why not?

MARY. Because I don't want you to, and because I can't stay here. I must get away.

EARLE. And where will you go?

MARY. I don't know.

EARLE. I think I shall have to follow you, and see how you fare.

MARY. You would spoil your pretty clothes.

EARLE. I have spoilt my pretty clothes more than once ere this.

MARY. That must have distressed your mother.

EARLE. My mother was in no situation to be distressed by a thing like that. She died when I was two.

MARY. You were fortunate.

EARLE. Do you think so? Don't you think she might have made a man of me?

MARY. Perhaps. You've made a queer sort of man of yourself.

[20]

EARLE.   Sir, when you have had longer experience in the task of creating your own manhood you will be more generous with other people's failures.

MARY.   What do you mean by that?

EARLE.   From the age of two until the age of twelve I was brought up by my father.   He taught me nothing but the feel of a hunting-crop on my back.   From the age of twelve till the age of twenty-one I served his Blessed Majesty King William III upon his oceans.   What the sea could teach me I have learnt.   I can read the stars and set a course for everyone but myself.

MARY.   Could you set a course for me?

EARLE.   I should need to know more about you, William.   Perhaps I shall some day.

MARY.   You don't look like a sailor.

EARLE.   I am not covered with tar.   I have the full complement of legs and I have two eyes.   Perhaps I am not a very satisfying sailor but I have followed the sea in my fashion.

MARY.   Not in the fashion in which you follow your art?

EARLE.   Yes.   Pretty much in the same fashion. I wasn't a very good sailor.   But you may have noticed this much of my old trade about me; I am very simple and a little mad.

MARY.   Yes.   I see that.   Shall I go to sea?

[EARLE *stops cleaning brushes.*]

EARLE.   Not if you wish to be your own master.   And that, it seems to me, is the most important thing anyone can want.

MARY.   Then shall I go to the wars?

EARLE.   You are no more likely to be your own master there.   And if I am to follow you, I'd as lief you chose somewhere safer.

MARY.   Are you afraid?

EARLE.   Yes, I am.

[SPANNER *enters* R.]

[21]

SPANNER. Ha. Our young pupil and the paint-slinger. Where is Theodora?

EARLE (*going*). Your servant, sir.

SPANNER. And yours, my good man. Ha! I thought to have the pleasure of seeing the great artist at his labours. And how does the pretty daub progress?

EARLE. Tolerably, sir.

SPANNER. You are a tall fellow to be getting your living by flattering females. Rot me, I've a mind to make a soldier of you.

EARLE. It is kind of you, sir, but I am not ambitious to be a soldier.

SPANNER. No, faith. I should think not. I was merely jesting with you, Sirrah.

EARLE. I see. Ha, ha!

SPANNER. What's that?

EARLE. A slight appreciation of your jest, sir. I wish you good-day.

[*He bows and goes.*]

SPANNER. Rot me if I can understand women. Half the females in the town are gone mad over that affected young rat. It would be a good act to give their Adonis a public beating some day. Begad, I'll do it when I have the leisure. . . . (*Hums . . . reclines on day-bed* R.) Where is Theodora?

MARY. She has gone to make herself beautiful, for you.

SPANNER. A labour of Hercules, by Gad! Rot her merry lungs. (*He sprawls on a day-bed* R. *and eats comfits.*) You are in high favour, that the old trot let you bring a mucky strap into her Highness's boudoir.

MARY. It isn't a mucky strap. It's Merrylegs' surcingle. It needs an extra hole or two. If she'd feed the poor jade and put some beef on her ribs, I shouldn't have to make fresh holes once a week.

SPANNER. Aye, aye. 'Tis a parsimonious old trot.

MARY (*rises*). You should be the last to say so.

SPANNER. I give value for value received. Do you think it gives me any pleasure to dance attendance on an antique figure of fun with a face to frighten the French? Never you make yourself an old wife's darling, William. I give you that piece of advice as a friend.

MARY. I am no friend of yours, Captain Spanner.

SPANNER. Hoity-toity, what's this? Am I not good enough for your worship? Am I not your friend, Will?

MARY. No.

SPANNER. Stap me, puppy.

MARY. If I were seeking a friend, I should look for a more manly sort of rogue.

SPANNER. Stap me, Will, I cannot have heard you correctly. What did you say?

MARY. I cannot understand my grandmother either. If I were an old woman I should see that my mangy lapdog was house-trained.

SPANNER. This is insufferable. I've had the ears . . .

MARY. I should have thought it was. But you seem to have a strong stomach for indignities.

SPANNER. Will, you are not yourself. Don't speak to me like that, lad.

MARY (*rises*). I have no wish to speak to you at all. I have learned a few bully's tricks from you and you can teach me no more. I have been heartsick of you for a week.

SPANNER. Now, now, Will!

MARY. I should be happiest if you would take yourself out of here.

SPANNER. So that's the game, is it? You want all the old trot's money for yourself. I'm your enemy, am I?

MARY. Yes!

SPANNER. Then you shall find what sort of an enemy Archy Spanner can be. You ask a certain platoon of Dutchmen what they think of a certain English captain as a blood-letter.

[23]

MARY. Blood-sucker, you mean.

SPANNER. Blood and wounds, that settles it! (*He draws his sword.*) Say your prayers, you hound.

> [MARY *beats down his guard with the surcingle and closes with him ; throws him back on the divan and begins to throttle him. He drops his sword and clutches her wrists.*]

God! Let go! You're choking me. You murderer! Theodora! Ah!

> [MARY *releases him, throws his sword into the fireplace and begins to beat him with the surcingle.*]

MARY. Take that, you creeping woman-queller, you dirty thief, you dog.

SPANNER. Oh, spare me! I can't bear it. I forgive you. Help! Help! Theodora!

> [*Enter precipitately,* OLD MRS. READ *and the* MAID.]

OLD MRS. R.⎫ Help! Murder! Thieves! Rape! Fire!
MAID.   ⎬ Let him go, Sir!

OLD MRS. R. What is the meaning of this?

SPANNER. I had only passed the time of day with him when he flew at me like a tiger. He is mad. Call the watch. Keep him away from me.

OLD MRS. R. Lysander, my precious. Are you injured?

SPANNER. What? Dreadfully. He has broken my wishbone.

OLD MRS. R. Cecily, run and fetch some arnica. Shall we get the doctor, sweetheart?

SPANNER (*rising*). No, no, no. It is nothing.

> [MAID *goes.*]

He took me unawares.

OLD MRS. R. Would you like to take him down to the courtyard and correct him with a horsewhip?

[24]

SPANNER. (MARY *picks up strap.*) No, no, no! It was nothing. He is a credit to my training. I like a lad of spirit, stap me.

OLD MRS. R. Generous soul.

SPANNER. And now, my Theodora must forgive me. I have an appointment.

OLD MRS. R. But you have only just arrived.

SPANNER. No. It is a matter of some urgency.

OLD MRS. R. We shall see you in the evening.

SPANNER. No. Perhaps. Yes. Oh, certainly. Farewell.

OLD MRS. R. I shall never forgive myself . . .

SPANNER. It is nothing. Farewell.

[SPANNER *hurries out.*]

OLD MRS. R. (*coming back*). And now, young sir?

MARY. Yes, Grandmamma?

OLD MRS. R. I think Captain Spanner has been deplorably weak. He should have whipped you within an inch of your life. I hope you realise what an escape you have had.

MARY. I am deeply grateful for it, Madam!

OLD MRS. R. A dangerous fighter like the Captain must have exercised *iron* self-control to avoid spitting you like a pullet.

[MAID *enters with arnica and bandages.*]

Take 'em away. The Captain has gone.

MARY. And you had better take his sword too. He may call for it. After I have left.

MAID. Oh, thank you, sir.

[*She takes the sword and goes.*]

OLD MRS. R. I don't understand.

MARY. I wish you would. I was at some trouble to thrash your white-livered poodle to make you understand what manner of man he is.

[25]

OLD MRS. R.   You *beat* Captain Spanner ?

MARY.   I thought that was sufficiently obvious.

OLD MRS. R.   How dared you ?   How dared you ?

MARY.   It didn't require much daring.

OLD MRS. R.   Poor Archy!   You dared to beat my friend ?

MARY.   Oh, Madam, cut the wretch out of your life.   He is unworthy of you.   I know it is hard for you, Madam.   I know perhaps better than you think.   It is sad to be lonely and old, and self-deception and vanity are a great solace to a woman, but . . .

OLD MRS. R.   I am not lonely.   I am not old.   What brute of a highwayman have I taken into my house. (*Smacks her face and kicks her.* MARY *has fallen on to the ground.*)

MARY (*rises*).   Very good, Madam.

> [*She takes a watch and a few coins from her pockets and lays them on the table.*]

OLD MRS. R.   What are you doing ?

MARY.   These are some money and the watch you gave me.

OLD MRS. R.   It was your grandfather's watch.

MARY.   I am already sufficiently beholden to him and to you.

OLD MRS. R.   Is that all the money you have ?

MARY.   Yes, Madam.

OLD MRS. R.   It isn't very much.

MARY.   You didn't give me very much, Madam.

OLD MRS. R.   How do you propose to live ?

MARY.   I don't know, Madam.

OLD MRS. R.   You will get into bad ways.   You will be a highwayman.

MARY.   Perhaps.   From what I have seen of gentlemen of fashion I would rather be a highwayman.

OLD MRS. R.   But you will be hanged.   My grandson hanged !

[26]

MARY. Very possibly, Madam.

OLD MRS. R. Or 'list for a soldier.

MARY. I had some such idea.

OLD MRS. R. God a'mercy, this is worse than the gripes. Oh, you impudent dog. Oh, you scandalising, tatterdemalion, poxy-faced ingrate! I take a clumsy lout of a strumpet's brat into my house—God save my soul alive, a pretty object of art and of virtue for a gentlewoman's boudoir you are, to be sure. Cecily, Cecily, bring me some cordial and some lavender water to my bedroom. I shall be sweating between the sheets for a week and all because of you. I feed you like a prize pig. I have you taught all the accomplishments of a gentleman. And do I get a word of thanks? Do I get a word of thanks?

MARY. (*politely*). Thank you, Madam, very much. Good-bye.

[*She bows and goes, jumping over stool.*]
[OLD MRS. R. *collapses weeping on stool back to audience.*]

CURTAIN

ACT I

SCENE III

A room opening off the tap-room in an ordinary at Dover. The door to the tap-room is open and a crowd of soldiers and civilians is seen within, drinking and listening to the end of a song. Another door gives on the open street.

At a table, littered with papers and recruiting ribbons, a SERGEANT *is refreshing himself with a mug of ale. On a bench near the door a one-legged* SAILOR *is doing likewise. The* SERGEANT *is doing a laborious bit of writing on a paper containing a long list of names.*

SERGEANT.   You'll excuse me for a minute, chum?

SAILOR.   Surely, mate, surely.

A VOICE.   Take a look at this, me lucky lads, take a look at this.   If you don't speculate you won't accumulate. Win a full house and drive in your carriage and pair. Shut that blasted door!   It's as cold as hell!

ANOTHER V.   Hell's not cold.

LOTTO PLAYER.   Oh, it ain't.   Then for why do they keep the fire burning continually?   Come along, my lucky lads. . . . *Shut that door!* . . . Heads down.   Luck in.

SAILOR.   Enjoying theirselves.

SERGEANT.   Yes, poor badgers.

VOICES.   Are we downhearted?

ANOTHER V.   *No!*

SERGEANT.   Well, you bloody soon will be!

[*The door is shut.*]

SAILOR.   Hech, hech!

SERGEANT.   No, honest chum. I'm sorry for them. You ain't seen what I've seen.   I'll tell you what it is. I should never drink ale when I'm on this recruiting job.

[28]

SAILOR. Because why?

SERGEANT. Because when I'm up to the neck in the Lord's gift to soldier men I can no more blarney a decent young man into taking the Queen's shilling than I'd chuck my own mother into the channel.

SAILOR. And it does you honour, Sergeant. The sentiment does you honour.

[*Knocks at hatch.* BARMAID *opens it.*]

VOICE OFF. Top o' the house. Legs eleven. Blind forty. Kelly's eye. Number ten.

SAILOR. Ahoy, sweetheart. Two more pints for the General and me.

[*Stumps down to below table again.*]
[*Young* OFFICER *enters door* C.]

OFFICER. Good-morning, Sergeant Bulwinkle.

SERGEANT. Good-morning, sir. I'm just closing the nominal roll. You'll have a fine upstanding draft to take out to the Colonel, sir. I wish I was going with them.

OFFICER. Well, it's time they were on board. I've been down to the packet, and the Captain's beginning to grumble about his tide.

SERGEANT. Very good, sir. Sergeant Jackson's in there, sir, with the men. Shall I go and tell him to get them fell in, sir?

OFFICER. No, I'll go in myself. I suppose we'd better close the nominal roll?

SERGEANT. Not likely to be any more, sir.

OFFICER. Very well. Bring the papers down to the ship. . . . I beg your pardon, Miss.

[*As he exits* R. *he barges into* BARMAID *entering with beer.* BARMAID *gives* SERGEANT *his, then down to*] SAILOR.]

BARMAID. Shall I chalk it up, Rumbo?

[29]

SAILOR.   Chalk it up, my darling.   (MARY *appears at window*.)   Hello, who have we here?

BARMAID.   Round by the other door, young sir.

MARY (*entering* C.)   I want to see the recruiting officer.

BARMAID.   There he is.   That's him there.

SERGEANT.   Well, my lad.   What is it?   Like to fall in and follow the drum?

MARY.   Yes.

[BARMAID *winks to* SAILOR *and exits* R.]

SERGEANT.   What did you say?

MARY.   I said " Yes "!   How should I set about it?

SERGEANT.   Why, blight me, anyone 'd think you were in earnest.

MARY.   I am in earnest, and I'm in a hurry.   How do I go for a soldier?   Quick!

[*She looks round anxiously.*]

SERGEANT.   See here, you.   Get home to yer ma, young fellow.

MARY.   You're a queer funny recruiting sergeant.

SERGEANT.   That's as may be.   Are you a page, or what?

MARY.   In a sort of a way.   I was a page to an old lady.   She's after me now, hell for leather, with a posse of armed stable-boys.   Let her be.   I've a mind to serve Queen Anne! so stir yourself and——

SERGEANT.   Eh, then, if there's likely to be trouble . . .

MARY (*back to table*).   I tell you I've a mind to serve Queen Anne.

SERGEANT.   Well, God bless 'er.   But I warn you, you'll find the Prince and Jack Churchill no easy masters. They'll fling you at a barricade as if you was cobblestones.

MARY.   And what of it?   If it pleases me, there's no reason for you to care.

SERGEANT.   *I* don't care, but I'm telling you all the same as I was telling this gentleman.   At Malpacket . . . Wasn't I just telling you? . . . There we was, me and a dozen others, up to our buttocks in muck. And no furder off nor you could spit, there was the Jacks spraying us with case-shot out of a blasted old bitch of a ten-pounder.

MARY. So you up and charged them?

SERGEANT. So we ups and *what*. There was a war on, young fellow. No, says I, you bug-bitten pack of weevils, I says, your heads ain't no use to you, but keep 'em down behind them gazons . . .

MARY. What are gazons?

SERGEANT. Gazons is soldier for them lousy deceiving clods of turf they called a breastwork when they sent us to hold it till furder orders, rot their eyesight. . . . Keep your heads down, says I, and by Satin, there we was, sucking muck, for the best part of an hour, when, rot my liver if it didn't come on to rain!

MARY. You should have charged them.

SERGEANT. Oh, I should have charged them, should I?

MARY. Yes. They were probably as big cowards as you.

SERGEANT. Sacrées tonnerres de guerre, my cockerel, you better have a care what you're . . . (*Bugle.*) If it weren't too late . . .

[BARMAID *and* MARY *run to window* L.]

MARY. Too late? For what? Are they falling in?

SERGEANT. They are. They'll be embarking in half an hour.

MARY. Write my name down there.

SERGEANT. Giving orders, are you?

MARY. Yes. My name's William Read. I'm nineteen . . .

SERGEANT. Take your time. How d'ye spell Read?

MARY. With an " a."

SERGEANT. Where's the " a " ?

[31]

MARY. R-E-A-D. Nineteen. Here, give it to me and be quick about it. . . . What about the oath? (*Pinning on a cockade.*)

SERGEANT. You'll need an officer for that. You can get him down at the ship if you're set on it.

MARY. I am. So come on. . . .

BARMAID. I wouldn't go if I was you. You don't need to go without you take the oath.

[EARLE *is seen outside window.*]

MARY. Come on.

[EARLE *enters door.*]

EARLE. Will, what are you doing here?

MARY. How did you get here? Are you one of the search party?

EARLE. No. What are you doing?

MARY. I'm 'listing myself into the Army. They don't seem to know how to do it here.

EARLE. Your grandmother's here with Spanner and a couple of armed grooms.

MARY. What?

EARLE. Yes.

WARNPANATROPE

BARMAID. Oh, mercy me. There'll be bloodshed.

[*Exit* R.]
[SAILOR *shuts window.*]
[*Two knocks.*]

SERGEANT (*after a pause*). Go round to the other door.

[*Knock.*]

SAILOR. Go round to the other door.

EARLE. Go round and round and make yourself dizzy. Yoicks!

SERGEANT (*coming out to* R. C. *below table*). If the lady's your lawful guardian. . . .

[32]

MARY (*front of table*). They can't take me. Come on, Ned. I'll put down your name too. There's room at the foot of the page. I'll make a man of you yet. Come on with me and fight the French.

EARLE. A soldier, me ? It would be madness to.

MARY. You told me yesterday you were mad.

EARLE. I'd rather be mad in my own way.

MARY. Is it a good way ?

EARLE. No, by God, it isn't.

MARY. Follow my fortune then.

[*Enter* BARMAID *in terror.*]

BARMAID. Sir, sir, I saw them in the tap-room.

SAILOR (*at window*). The troops are just marching out.

BARMAID. You'll only start a brawl in a decent house.

SERGEANT. She's quite right, you'd better renège.

MARY. No. It seems to be a hard business to fight for one's Queen, but by God I'll do it. Will you follow my fortune, Ned ?

EARLE. Yes, I'll follow your fortune and you ten thousand leagues to the world's end.

MARY. Good. (*Pushes* SERGEANT *over* C. *to* EARLE.)

EARLE. Give me the pen.

[SPANNER *and* two FOOTMEN *enter armed with blunderbusses.*]

SPANNER. Surrender in the Queen's name.

[MARY *picks up* SERGEANT's *pistols and levels them.*]

MARY. Who the hell are you to use the Queen's name ? I'm the Queen's man now. There's her Officer. Ask him. Ned, take their weapons.

[EARLE *takes blunderbusses and puts them on table.*]

You'd better tell your men not to struggle, Spanner. For two reasons.

[*She indicates the pistols.*]

D   [33]

Take the Sergeant's papers, Ned. (EARLE *goes over to table* L. *and gets papers from* SERGEANT.) Turn your faces to the wall. (*To* SPANNER *and* GROOMS.) Now, say your prayers.

> [EARLE *jumps up on window-sill. Gives* MARY *a hand up. As she gets up she fires first one pistol then the other.*]

CURTAIN *on first shot.*

> [*When the* CURTAIN *is coming down the* BAND (*Panatrope*) *has swelled to* FF. *and a mob cheer outside window.*]

ACT II

SCENE.—*A farmhouse in North-west Flanders. The scene shows a big living-room with a loft above it. The loft is reached by a staircase and a hatch and is open at the front. The place has been inhabited, but the inhabitants have left it recently and in haste. It is late afternoon in the autumn of* 1714.

EARLE, *in the tattered uniform of a light dragoon, enters hurriedly. He is covered with mud, he has lost his hat, and he looks desperately ill.*

EARLE. Marie Louise! . . . Hey! Marie Louise! . . . C'est moi! Ned Earle. Marie!

[*He staggers to the door, hears hoofs and looks out; jerks back in a panic; looks desperately for a place to hide; makes for the loft and buries himself under a heap of old clothes. Noise of hoof-beats near.*]

A VOICE. Walk, march. Halt. Prepare to dismount. Dismount. Look to your hosses.

[*Stamping and jangling of equipment.*]

SNYDE. Steady a minute, sir. There may be somebody inside.

[*Enter* CAPTAIN TAPPIT, *a stout, elderly officer, carrying a huge horse-pistol.*]

TAPPIT. Oh, rot that! It's as empty as Heaven, and a snug-looking billet too.

[TROOPER SNYDE *and* TROOPER OCKLES *follow him with carbines at the ready.*]

[35]

Put those carbines away.   We shan't want them.
There ain't a soul here. . . . Where's the Corporal?

SNYDE.   Corpril Read!   Captin wants ye.

A VOICE.   Corpril Read!

ANOTHER V.   Corpril Read!

MARY (*without*).   Coming along, sir!

TAPPIT.   Tell him to look lively.   Oddsfiggers, what
a day!

> [*He goes through a door to an inner room and re-enters
> almost immediately.*]

Good.   The room will serve very well.   There's
a bed, and the bugs didn't get up on their tails and give
three cheers for Prince Eugene as they did last night.
You needn't laugh, man.   That wasn't particularly
funny. (*Sits on steps.*)   Go fetch my saddle-bags,
Ockles.

> [*Exit* OCKLES.]

You, Snyde, there's a brazier in there.   Bring it in
here and light it up.   I'll billet some of the men here.
I won't have them sleeping in a pig-sty.   Where the
devil's the Corporal? . . . It's odd we should come on
a place like this empty. . . . It's been lived in during the
last few days.   There's a stink of *bruinbier* about it still.
. . . Where's the . . . ah, there you are, Corporal;
where the devil have you been?   (*Back to steps.*)

> [*Enter* MARY READ R. *in a smart dragoon uniform.*]

MARY.   Fixing the horse lines, sir.

TAPPIT.   Odslife, ain't the Sergeant capable of doing
that?

MARY.   No, sir.

TAPPIT.   Then what's he a sergeant for?

MARY.   I don't know, sir.

TAPPIT.   It's a comfort to find something you don't
know.   See here, you know this countryside?

[36]

MARY. Yes, sir. I rode over it with Ensign Brook last week. This place was occupied then, sir; but I have just learned that a party of Hessians were fired upon from the window last week . . . by franc-tireurs, sir.

TAPPIT. So it is no longer occupied, eh ?

MARY. The courtyard sump is, sir.

TAPPIT. I see. Brutes, those Hessians.

MARY. There's a weather-tight barn with dry straw, sir. It will hold the men comfortably. There's a good standing for the horses in the orchard. The pump's working all right. There's a good deal of iron in the water, but it's good for the blood, they say. The men had a good bellyful at the last halt, so I'm saving the rations for breakfast, and the cook is making some soup in the copper. I've posted a picket of four flying sentries and warned all reliefs, sir. I propose to sound stables in half an hour.

TAPPIT. So that's all you've done, is it ?

MARY. That's all, sir. Will you billet here, sir ? That'll do, Ned Snyde; look lively and tell Ockles he can bring his honour a bowl of soup presently. Shake yourself, now.

SNYDE. Very good, Corpril. I got something in my eye.

[SNYDE goes.]

TAPPIT. Beggar me, I believe you like soldiering, Will.

MARY (down blowing fire). It is well enough, sir.

TAPPIT. It's a rough life for a lad like you.

MARY. It's as you make it, sir.

TAPPIT. Damme, you're a gentleman, a gentleman.

MARY. I hope so, sir, but it is pleasant to hear you say so.

TAPPIT. You should be skipping it with the staff as an officer, you with your pretty voice and Nancy manners. (MARY gives T. a look.)

MARY. I have no money to buy a commission, sir.

[37]

TAPPIT. Tonnerre de guerre, that's a pity. You're a born leader. The men listen to you, not to me, blast 'em.

> [*Enter* OCKLES *and* SNYDE *with fuel and saddle-bags. They set about lighting a fire, and continue clearing.* OCKLES *takes the bag into the back room.*]

MARY. Do you want me for anything further, sir ?

TAPPIT. No. I don't think so. But you and the Sergeant and these two barrack-rats had better billet here. You won't disturb me. It'll take a canister bomb to my midriff to disturb me to-night.

MARY. Thank you, sir. I'll tell the Sergeant, sir.

> [*Salutes and exit.*]

TAPPIT (*singing*).
    Slaet op den trommele van dirre dom deyne.
    Slaet op den trommele van dirre doum, doum.

SNYDE. Beg pardon, sir.

TAPPIT. I was singing. That is a Flemish song, Snyde, my lad. It means " Beat up the drum " or something.   Do you know the language ?

SNYDE. Yes, sir. In a way of speaking. I know " C'est la guerre " and " Promenade avec." Just the necessaries, like.

OCKLES. Beg pardon, sir. Should I take a look up here ?

TAPPIT. Let it be. Leave the loft to the rats.

OCKLES. You don't think there'd be spies or anything; in hiding, like ?

TAPPIT. You take your ideas from me, my lad. Don't go getting any of your own.

> [*Enter* TROOP-SERGEANT CASEY, *a decrepit little man walking stiffly.*]

Ha ! Troop-Sergeant Casey. This is indeed a pleasure.

[38]

CASEY. All present and correct, sir.

TAPPIT. That's a comfort. And how do you find yourself, my dear?

CASEY. Ach, the Holy Saints know whether I'll see the blessed light of morning. I feel that bad.

TAPPIT. Odso. Well, you may bake the pains out of your bones against that stove. I'm going to bed.

CASEY. Any orders, sir?

TAPPIT. Orders? Orders? What the devil would you be doing with orders? Good-night, Sergeant.

CASEY. Good-night, Captain Tappit, sir.

OCKLES. And the soup, sir?

TAPPIT. Oh, damn the soup.

[Exits into room L.]

Ockles, come in with me and take off my boots.

CASEY (*puts down sword and hat against stair*). Oh, wirra, wirra, the sorrow's on me.

[Takes out a bottle. Drinks. About to give Snyde one too but changes his mind.]

Away wit you, ye omadhaun, and fetch me my blanket. Can't you see it's dying on my feet I am, like Lot's wife in the story?

SNYDE. Very good, Sergeant.

[He goes out R., *whistling " Lillibulero."]*
*[*OCKLES *enters* L., *whistling " Après la Guerre."]*

CASEY. Musha, is it a choir of blackbirds you think you are, filling the whole air around you with piercing sounds and a man at death's door? It's enough to drive a man crazy wit' the noise of it.

[He is huddled over the stove.]

OCKLES. I'm sorry, Sergeant. It was a tune came into my head.

[39]

CASEY.   Well, just you chase it out again.   This is no war to be whistling in.

OCKLES.   Roll on the time, eh, Sergeant ?

CASEY.   Faith, it's not in your time or my time the thing 'll come to an end, nor not till the living inhabitants of the wide earth 'll be lying stiff in their gore.

[*Enter* SNYDE *with a heap of blankets.* SERGEANT *takes all but one, followed by* MARY READ.]

. . . And there's yourself Corporal.

MARY.   And here's myself, Sergeant.   See, there's a bowl of hot soup for the chill on your belly.   Tom, you'd better get round to the cook-house and have a sup. Come back when you've had it.   You're to sleep here to-night.

OCKLES.   Very good, Corporal.

[*He goes out* R.   MARY *sits on stairs.*]

CASEY.   The pains of hell sit light on you, William. You're a Dutch uncle to me.   Have ye seen to the watering and grooming, now ?

MARY.   Make your mind easy.   There's a happy good-night in front for man and beast, and, God knows, I doubt if there's anything better *in this sad world.*

[*Men sing off* R. " *Lillibulero.*"]
[*She takes off her spurs.   A burst of song is heard from the barn where the troops are quartered.*]

The men are in good fettle to-night.

CASEY.   Ah, yes, poor fellows.   I do me best to keep their spirits up.   It's a living marvel to me the hearts in them don't break.   (SNYDE *snatches blanket.*)   Though if they'd of seen what I've seen . . .

MARY.   They break sometimes.   And it's a bad sight to see.

CASEY.   And that's no lie.   I remember well . . .

[MARY *rises.*]

[40]

CASEY. Och, rats in the attic. Holy Saints, the lep you gave. You're not yourself this night at all, at all.

MARY. Never you mind what I am. There are times you think war is a fine warm business with its order and its comradeship and the man-hunt and the danger, and then the boys riding knee to knee turn suddenly to a row of ugly puppets.

SNYDE. I wouldn't take it bad that way, Corpril. He ain't worth it, no more he ain't.

MARY. Who's not worth it?

CASEY. Now, now, now, Ned Snyde. Be more careful what you say.

MARY. Let him alone. Who's not worth it, you lousy dog?

SNYDE. Not meaning any offence, Corpril, why, Ned Earle.

MARY. Don't say that cowardly maggot's name to me, d'you hear?

SNYDE. No offence, Corpril.

MARY (*a quiet snivel*). Where does this stair lead?

SNYDE. Up to the loft.

MARY. Did you search the loft?

SNYDE. The Captain said we wasn't to trouble.

MARY. He did, did he? I'll sleep up there for a couple of hours. Tell the sentry where I am if I haven't awakened by then.

SNYDE. You'll wake all right, Corpril. You've got a clock in your head.

CASEY. Musha, why not sit by the fire a while and talk?

SNYDE (*sitting up*). I meant no offence what I said just now about Ned Earle. Seeing you 'listed together and he was your mate, like.

MARY. I've told you before, if I meet that white-livered hound I'll kill him with my two hands. A deserter is no mate of mine.

CASEY. Och, the poor lad wasn't the make of a

[41]

soldier. Poor fellow. You've a hard cruel heart, William.

[*Enter* OCKLES R.]

MARY. That's as may be. Did you get your soup, Tom ?

OCKLES. Aye. The lads are getting into the hay. They're dog-tired.

MARY. You get down to it too. Good-night.

[MARY *mounts the ladder to the loft, carrying her spurs, a blanket and a candle. The loft is lit by moonlight. The stage is nearly dark except for the glow from the stove.*

The three men settle themselves round it, wrapped in their blankets. MARY *takes off her equipment and tunic, straps her sword to her wrist, sticks a pistol in her right boot, and lies down to sleep. Puts light out.*]

CASEY. A strange one, that.

SNYDE. Hey ? What did you say ?

CASEY. A mighty queer one is William.

SNYDE. Oh. Good-night.

CASEY. There'd be nobody less surprised than myself would be if you was to tell me he was changed in his cradle by the fairies. There was a lad by the name of MacDonald that served with him in the P.B.I. that was telling me he saw with his own eyes the bullets spreading to a circle round him and him going forward loike he was in a moving tunnel of lead. I've often had that in me mind when I've been tempted to put that lad in his place. (*Yawn.*) It's bad enough luck there is in these wars wit'out crossing one o' the good people.

OCKLES. I don't know nothing about good people and such, but he's a mucky fine soldier.

CASEY. And what in the living world does the like of you know about soldiering ? It's the curse on me I wasn't killed myself years ago, but I'm saying I t'ink

I'm the only rale soldier left in this crucified army. (*Yawn.*) That's the worst of a long war. In Spain, now, in '95 . . .

SNYDE. For God's sake, go to sleep.

[*Rolls over round fire.*]

CASEY. That's the worst of ye, Ned Snyde, ye won't listen and ye'll never learn, no, not if the holy Saints themselves was to come down from heaven and give ye a choice selection from their most interesting experiences.

OCKLES. *Good-night, Sergeant.*

CASEY. Oh, good-night to you, *Mr. Thomas Ockles, Esquire,* and pleasant dreams to you, and may the devil make garters o' yer guts.

[*Silence. The firelight dims a little and the moonlight grows.* MARY, *to the astonishment of the audience, begins to whimper quietly. This grows presently to a gale of good, honest, choking womanish sobs. This betrays the fugitive* EARLE *into a movement.* MARY *leaps to her feet and twitches the covering off him.*]

MARY (*in a husky whisper, still uneven with sobbing*). Get up!

[EARLE *gets up ; they look at one another.*]

So it's you, Ned Earle.

EARLE. Yes.

[*A pause.*]

MARY. Get down that stair.

EARLE. What do you mean ?

MARY. I said I'd have no mercy if I ever saw you again. Get down that stair.

EARLE. I'm ill. I've been hit. I can hardly stand. Can't you see that I'm ill ?

MARY. What do I care ? Do as I tell you.

EARLE. I'm done. Let me rest. . . .

[43]

MARY. You'll rest in hell in a second. Do you want me to blow a hole through your ribs?

EARLE. You can't do it. You can't give me up. I'm finished. Listen to me. Just for a moment.

MARY. What can you have to say? You're a coward and a traitor.

EARLE. I know that. Have pity on me. I couldn't go on. Two years of it. Two years of marching and riding and sleeping with cold fear. I'm not a fighting man. You know that. I had to levant. You can't do it. I tell you you can't . . .

MARY. Keep quiet, you fool. Do you want the men to hear you? (*A pause.*)

EARLE. Then you won't . . .? You'll try to save me?

MARY. It's too late for that. How did you get here?

EARLE. My mare went lame and I sold her. I walked the rest. There was a girl here I knew. I thought she'd hide me, but she'd gone.

MARY. Why didn't you trust me? I was your comrade. I'd have helped you through. That's what comrades are for.

EARLE. You could never understand. It was the same when I served at sea. Up to a point I could hold the pretence. Then it broke. . . . I had better fortune then. Now . . . I can't think. I can't breathe. I can only run till I drop.

MARY. You can breathe enough now to talk like a mill-race.

EARLE. I'm better. Now I'm with you. I'm better.

MARY. It's a pity you didn't think of me before instead of running to your doxy. . . .

EARLE. I tell you I . . .

MARY (*savagely*). It may please you to know that her body's in the sump in the courtyard, with her throat cut and . . .

EARLE.   Oh, no! Don't. Don't speak like that. . . .
Oh, God, how could you do it?

MARY.   We didn't do it. But that's the way to treat
dirty spies.

EARLE.   She wasn't a spy; she . . .

MARY.   And you can join your sweetheart that you
love so dearly . . .

EARLE.   I didn't. . . . She wasn't . . .

MARY.   And you can lie with her in the sump to-night
and rot.

EARLE.   You are a fiend. You're mad. What is
the matter with you? Oh, kill me and have done with
it. (*Flops down head on her lap.*)

MARY.   Ned. Don't do that. Hush, Ned. I'll
save you. Hush, don't cry. You're safe, Ned.

EARLE.   God knows I'm not, but I feel safe. That's
the strange thing about it. . . . You make us feel safe."

MARY.   What do you say, Ned? Who make you
feel safe?

EARLE.   If you're on the edge of death itself and
you know it, they still make you feel safe.

MARY.   What are you talking about? Who make
you feel safe?

EARLE (*pause*).   Women make you feel safe.

MARY.   What do you mean?

EARLE.   Why do you think I left my paint-brushes
and my coffee-houses to follow this death in life?

MARY.   Then you knew?

EARLE.   Yes.

MARY.   How long have you known?

EARLE.   When I told your fortune in your grandmother's house, I knew.

MARY.   But why didn't you . . . So you knew all
the time?

EARLE.   God bless you, if I hadn't known and helped
to guard your secret, do you think you'd have kept it
for a week?

[45]

MARY. You're not like other men. I think that's why I took you with me and why I wanted to kill you and why I can't.

[MARY *breaks down.*]

EARLE. There, there, keep on crying, my darling. Lord, the weeks and months you've kept that pent up in your heart, and all the time you've never had a breast to weep on and no one to tell you he loves you. Why do you run away from such things?

MARY. I don't know.

EARLE. It's a worse thing to run away from that than my poor running away from war. What is your name, your real name?

MARY. Mary.

EARLE. Mary. . . . Are you still afraid of being a woman?

MARY. No. I was never afraid. But I hated them, and what they did and said, and thought but didn't say. This is not like that.

EARLE. Why were you crying just now?

MARY. I felt lonely.

EARLE. You will never be lonely again.

[*Long pause.*]

MARY. Do you love me?

EARLE. I love you. (*They kiss.*)

MARY. Stop. Let me go. . . . No . . . let me go. I must think. Oh, my darling, what are we to do?

EARLE. You know what there is to do. There is nothing else in the world but . . .

MARY. No, I must keep my head. You must get away. . . .

EARLE. Not yet. Oh, not yet.

[*A long embrace. He puts her over to* R. *She nestles on his* R. *shoulder.*]

MARY. What will you do if you escape to England? You can't stay in England.

EARLE. I'll go to the Indies. My brother is a merchant in the Indies. And you will quit this wild business and wrap petticoats round your legs and come to me in Pernambuco.

MARY. Pernambuco? What sort of a place is that?

EARLE. It's the port of Brazil. A fine town, my brother tells me, with broad tiled pavements, and great avenues of tall cocoanut trees, and the sun shines all day long. There's a bridge of twenty-eight arches and a stinking huge bazaar, and little green parrots fly about the streets. They dig out dark, copper-coloured gold, and mint it into moidores. My brother trades in sugar and tobacco. He sent me once a quintal-roll soaked in molasses and smelling of caramel-earth. A strange smell. It carried me into a dream of purple mountains and dark trailing jungles.

MARY. Pernambuco? I'll remember that. You'll wait for me?

EARLE. I owe you my life. I love you.

[*After a short pause there is a loud knock at the door* R. SERGEANT CASEY *and* OCKLES *and* SNYDE *at once rouse themselves.*

CASEY. What in the name of God is it? Is it the French at all? (*Goes out* R.)

[*Another knock.* SNYDE *arouses* TAPPIT, L., *then goes out* R.]

EARLE. That's the end. They'll find me.

MARY. Keep still. There's only one way now. I think they're after you. You must take a chance and get through the window. Then drop on to the outhouse roof and run like the devil for the horse-lines. You'll see the storm-lamp by the edge of the orchard. Make for it.

EARLE. I daren't, I daren't.

[47]

MARY. Don't break my heart. I'll tell you when to start.

[*They cower down as* TAPPIT *enters* L., *struggling with a boot, and his sword loose in his hand.*]

TAPPIT. What the devil. . . . Hey, Corporal Read! Sergeant! Where is everybody?

[*As he reaches the door* R. *he meets a* LIFEGUARDSMAN.]

Who the devil are you?

LIFEGUARD. Provost Marshal's picket, sir. The civilian out there, sir, interrupted Sir George in the middle of his dinner, to tell him the deserter Ned Earle had been seen entering this house.

TAPPIT (*coming further in*). And what the devil has that got to do with me? I was asleep, don't you realise?

LIFEGUARD. Can't help it, sir. We've got to make a search.

TAPPIT. Zounds, where is Corporal Read?

LIFEGUARD. With your permission, sir, I'll start with the attic. (*To door.*) Cantwell, Margerson, Hawkes! Never mind these damned things. Come along. We can't wait here all night.

[LIFEGUARD, TAPPIT *exit* R. *and a noise of voices is heard. As soon as* MARY *realises that the coast is for a moment clear she speaks.*]

MARY. Now's your chance. Take this.

[*She gives* EARLE *her pistol and helps him half-way through the little window. A shot is fired and* EARLE *falls back into the room.*]

A VOICE. We got him, Lieutenant.

[*The* LIFEGUARDSMAN *runs out.* MARY *gives a strangled cry and falls on* EARLE's *body.*]

TAPPIT (*entering* R.). That was a woman's cry.

OCKLES. Sounds like it, sir.

[*He goes to the foot of the steps. The room fills with soldiers.*]

LIFEGUARD. Up the stairs, there. He was shot at the attic window. Be careful. He may be armed.

[MARY *rises quickly and goes to the stairs. She is half-way down before the Marshal's men reach the lower step.*]

MARY. There's blood on his face! He's covered with blood. He couldn't speak to me. He's dead! I love him so! Why did they do that? He didn't hurt them. He was afraid . . . (*shouting*) . . . You've killed my husband! You murderers! Damn you, you bloody murderers!

[*She falls in a faint.*]

CURTAIN

ACT II

SCENE II

A disreputable tavern in Cheapside. There are two short crazy flights of stairs, the one on the right leading to the street, the other on the left to an inner room. The one-legged sailor of Act I is the Landlord of the dive. He is telling a story to two sluts who sit gazing at him in rapt attention. Glasses which have contained gin are in front of them.

RUMBO. I'm not saying it's gospel, but they say he was a trooper two years ago.

SLUT (1). Who was?

RUMBO. The cove I'm telling about. This ruddy artist.

SLUT (1). Which artist?

RUMBO. Him with the hole in his head and the bad temper.

SLUT (1). All right. You don't have to shout.

RUMBO. Then listen.

SLUT (2). Be quiet. Go on, Rumbo.

RUMBO. Well, 'e went to the wars in Flanders, and he took his doxy with him, dressed as a trooper like himself, breeks an' all.

SLUT (1). 'E's one for his home comforts then?

SLUT (2). And didn't they ever rumble what she was?

RUMBO. Never. Till one day the artist tried to desert the service, and got shot in his darling's arms.

SLUT (1). Was 'e killed?

SLUT (2). How could he be, when he comes in here like Rumbo's telling you?

[50]

SLUT (I). An' how did they find out she was a woman?

RUMBO. They had a court-martial, and she had to tell. But she begged a pardon for him and got him off. Then she left the army, sets up in a little beer-house where she served the troops and nursed him back to life.

SLUT (I). Lovely. Some more gin, Rumbo.

RUMBO. But she might have saved herself the trouble.

SLUT (2). Why?

RUMBO. Because he's no sooner out of his bandages than he ups anchor.

SLUT (I). Left her d'ye mean?

RUMBO. High and dry.

SLUT (2). The low hound.

RUMBO. And you can see him here any day. His workshop's hard by, and though he's got money to burn he'd sooner drink here than with the gentry. Makes him feel less sick he says.

[*The anabaptist has been sitting at Table* R. *as if asleep.*]

ANABAPTIST (*waking and rising* R.). Oh, Sodom and Gomorrah.

SLUT (I). Them's not our names, dearie. This is Poll, an' I'm Clara.

ANA. (*crossing*). Woe and lamentation.

SLUT (2) (*helping him to lie down*). Put this in your gob and lie quiet.

RUMBO. Stow it you. What's the matter with him?

SLUT (2). He's all right. He was at the hanging this afternoon at Tyburn, and it's gone to his head.

RUMBO. Did you have a pleasant execution, my darlings?

SLUT (2). Lovely. Right up against the cart-wheel I was.

SLUT (I). I never had a better view in my life. I saw the rope put round his neck, and heard his last grunt.

RUMBO.   So poor Tom had a good end?

SLUT (1).   Indeed he did.   Drunk as a judge he was. His last dram was running out of the corners of his mouth.

> [*Enter* MRS. READ *carrying a basket of goods, including a water-melon.   She has degenerated since she was last seen, but still retains a remnant of coquetry.*]

MRS. READ.   Good afternoon, Landlord.

RUMBO.   Good afternoon to you, Mistress.   Your Lord and master was bawling for you a minute agone.

MRS. READ.   Oh?   What does he want?

RUMBO.   You should know better nor me.

> [SPANNER *appears at top of steps* U.L. *drunk and dishevelled.*]

SPANNER.   Where is everybody?   Am I to get no service in this damned case-house?   Archy Spanner's cut the ears off a man before now, aye, and salted them and made him eat them.   (MRS. READ *laughs.*)   Oh, there you are, Hannah, you slut.

MRS. READ.   I brought you a nice water-melon, Archy dear.   Here, I'll cut it for you.

> [*Gets plate and knife from bar.   Cuts melon at table* D.R.]

SPANNER.   Water-melon?   Do you think I'm a stinking Jamaica black, rot me?

MRS. READ.   Now you'll take it.   It's very nice and cool and 'll take the horrid taste out of your mouth.

SPANNER.   How do you know what my mouth tastes like?   (*Laugh.*)   Get me a noggin of spirits.

MRS. READ.   Get Captain Spanner a noggin of spirits, Landlord.

SAILOR.   Now these young ladies here will tell you that I'm a generous-hearted man, but . . .

MRS. READ.   Can't you see the poor lamb's not well? Here's a slice of melon for you, Archy, and I'm sure the

[52]

kind landlord will bring you a little aquavitæ presently. It's his heart, Landlord. (*Crosses down to* RUMBO.)

CLARA (*1st slut*). Well, I must be goin'! Mercy, I forgot old Holy Joe.

POLL (*2nd slut*). He's asleep. Let 'im be.

[*The* SLUTS *have a row over him.* SAILOR *separates them.*]

SAILOR. Go on, get out.

1ST SLUT. Come along, Poll.

2ND SLUT. I'm coming. Good-day to you, Mrs. Spanner.

[*They both go out* R.]

MRS. READ (*down to* RUMBO, L.C.). I think you might have more consideration for a lady and gentleman born than to force them to associate with the like of that.

SAILOR. Oh, they're good girls. A lady like you that's secure in her own virtue need never bother her head about them. (*Pinches her.*)

MRS. READ. That's true enough.

SAILOR. A noggin of spirits, I think you said?

MRS. READ. You might make it two, if it's all the same. Come, darling, we'll retire to our apartment. Oh, I've forgotten the melon.

[*She assists* SPANNER *into the back-room and returns quickly to take the brandy from the* SAILOR.]

Who was the gentleman that girl was speaking about?

SAILOR. Mr. Earle, the painter.

MRS. READ. Ah, I know. Poor young fellow. If I could do him any good by talking to him . . . Sometimes refined female society . . . And it might keep him out of . . . well . . . harm's way. . . . (*Going up steps.*)

SAILOR. I'll keep you in mind, Ma'am.

[53]

MRS. READ. Thank you, Landlord.

> [*She retires into the back-room.*]
> [SAILOR *sings a rough sea song.*]
> [MARY READ *enters* R. *dressed as a woman in black.*]

MARY. Is this Rumbo Bill's lodging?

SAILOR. The very spot, Ma'am.

MARY. Does Mrs. Read live here?

SAILOR (*bottom of table* L.). She does, Ma'am.

MARY. God have mercy. Who are you?

SAILOR. I'm the landlord, Ma'am.

MARY. I've seen you before.

SAILOR. Is that so, Ma'am? I don't recollect your face. But then I've seen a mort of faces tacking about the seven seas.

MARY. Where's Mrs. Read?

SAILOR. Ahoy there, Mistress! Here's a lady to see you.

> [*He goes behind bar—out* C. *opening.*]
> [*Enter* MRS. READ.]

MRS. READ. Yes? (MARY *rises.*) For Mercy's sake!!

MARY. Well, Mother?

MRS. READ. Where did you spring from?

MARY. You've changed, Mother. Why are you here? In this place?

MRS. READ. Where have you been? You look spick and span, but you're thinner.

MARY. I've been looking for you for months. I thought I should never find you. Are you in want, Mother? Do you need help?

MRS. READ. Of course I do. Do you think I would live in this horrible place for choice? Sit down, girl, and let me look at you. (*Indicates seat* L. *of table.*)

MARY. I thought I had better come back to you, Mother.

MRS. READ. When did you give up being a boy?
Did you find a man?

MARY. Yes. I found a man.

MRS. READ. Couldn't you keep him? After all I
taught you?

MARY. No. I couldn't keep him.

MRS. READ. So you're back to your ma?

MARY. Yes.

MRS. READ. And what am I to do with you. Have
you any money?

MARY. I've got a little money . . . Mother, you
were in the right of it. I've come back. You must
teach me to be a woman again. (*Sits beside* MRS. READ.)

MRS. READ. I'll do that all right, if you can pay for
your lesson . . . you find me in somewhat reduced
circumstances, poppet. How much money have you
got?

MARY. We shall have to find work. Though God
knows what I'm fit for but a female turnkey at Newgate.

MRS. READ. Oh, I don't know. You have come
back quite personable, my dear. And when we have
rid you of that horrible sunburn. . . . How much
money did you say you had?

MARY. I have ninety pounds.

MRS. READ. It is not very much among three of us.

MARY. Three?

MRS. READ. Yes. I have a little good news for you,
but that will keep. Now, let me see—we must put our
thinking caps on. If we were to make a good show of it
and move to a refined lodging, and put down fifty pounds
of it as earnest of a dowry. . . . The only thing is to
find the man. Well, my protector, in a new suit of
clothes, could search the coffee-houses. . . . It is high
time he did some work, and . . . oh, there is much that
could be done with ninety pounds, wisely invested.

MARY. Mother, Mother, I had thought of finding
some honest work.

MRS. READ. And what profit do you suppose is in honest work? No, no! You have landed us all in a pretty pickle. You must trust to my wits and experiences of the world. . . . Ha! Perhaps we need hardly invest so *much* of our little capital. A gentleman who comes here sometimes . . . well-connected . . . pays his way. I must have a talk to the gentleman. The ways of Providence are inscrutable indeed.

[SPANNER *appears at the door, eating melon.*]

SPANNER. What about another noggin of . . . (*Down to* C.) My service to you, Madam. I'm sorry, Hannah; I did not know you were receiving company.

MRS. READ. I don't know . . . I thought perhaps you two . . . no, I forgot. You haven't met before.

SPANNER. Better late than never, stap me. You find us in poor quarters, Ma'am, but an old soldier like myself is used to rough lodging. Would the lady enjoy some cordial, Hannah? We might perhaps join her.

[MRS. READ *comes round between them.*]

MRS. READ. Captain Spanner, this is my niece Mary. I think I told you of her. She was companion to a Countess in the north country. She desires a change of occupation and taste of the gaieties of city life.

SPANNER. I shall be honoured, by Gad, to be her cicerone.

[*At this moment* EARLE *stumbles down the outer steps and slowly, as if not seeing the others, makes his way over to the table. The* SAILOR *comes out of his den behind the bar.* EARLE *raps on the table with his cane.*]

EARLE. Landlord!

SAILOR. Ah, your Honour. (*Nudges* MRS. READ *in passing and indicating* EARLE *with a knowing leer.*) It's

a sight for sore eyes to see you again, sir. I thought
we'd lost you. The usual, sir?

> [MRS. READ *drops* D.S. *to have a good look at* EARLE. SAILOR
> *again winks to her.*]

EARLE. The usual, and don't jabber at me to-day,
pray. My head aches.

SAILOR. Certainly, your Honour. (*Goes to fetch
bottle and glass.*)

SPANNER. Hey, while you're about it . . .

MRS. READ. Hush, Archy, it's the gentleman who . . .
Oh, I'm all in a flutter.

SPANNER (*crosses and lies over table* L.). A pleasant
afternoon, sir, for the season of the year. If you are so
pressing, I should like to join you in a convivial glass . . .

EARLE. Sir, I have no wish for your society. Do
me the honour to take yourself . . . why, I've seen
you before.

> [MRS. READ *has got round to* L. *of table.*]

SPANNER. Well, sir, in that case . . . why, it's
the pretty artist. Rot my lungs, what an encounter.
This positively calls for a glass. Hey, Landlord. I
little thought to see you again. What became of you
after you fell in behind the flag with our young Willy
Read?

> [LANDLORD *comes out with bottle.* EARLE *strikes him with
> his cane. He sets up a cry of* "Murder" *and the
> SAILOR *comes in.*]

MRS. READ. You must not mind him, sir. He is
very injudicious. He is always getting beaten. Archy,
go into your room. You're a very . . .

> [EARLE *follows the slinking figures with his eyes and
> recognises* MARY READ.]

EARLE. So you have found me.

MRS. READ. So you know each other?

MARY. Yes. We know each other. Through and through.

MRS. READ. How . . . how fortunate. I hope . . .

MARY. Will you go, please, to your—your lover, and leave us alone ?

MRS. READ. My poppet, of course, if Mr. Earle will excuse us. With old friends one need not keep too strictly to the letter of the proprieties, need one ? Perhaps Mr. Earle will join us later in a . . . in a . . . collation.

[*She fades through the doorway.*]

MARY. So you are not afraid of Archy Spanner now ? That at least is something.

EARLE. Don't talk like that! Don't talk like that to me! (*Leans head against mantelpiece.*)

MARY. How should I talk to you ? Shall I thank you for being a faithful husband and a loyal friend ?

EARLE. No. Talk as you wish. I can feel nothing now.

MARY. I think you could feel nothing at any time, ever.

EARLE. You think that, do you ?

MARY. I befriended you. I helped you. I gave you what I could. I . . .

EARLE. And now you come to me in my peaceful gutter where I sit among the cabbage leaves and upbraid me like a fishwife ? Can you not leave me alone ?

MARY. What sort of man are you ?

EARLE. The sort of man you made me . . . my sweet!

MARY. I made you ?

EARLE. Yes. . . . I was an artist and a philosopher,— I had found a way of living. I was gentle and indifferent and happy. You see me now with my body and my soul broken; and my nerves writhing like a bag of serpents round a core of insufferable misery. Look at me, yes, look at me! Admire the lines and the hollows and all the rest of the exquisite workmanship; and then, by God, take the picture and sign it, for it's yours!

MARY.   You can talk as well as ever.

EARLE.   Much better.

MARY.   Whoever made you, made you a snarling coward from your birth. . . . And what have you done to me?

EARLE.   Nothing.

MARY.   You've tricked me into being a woman again.

EARLE.   I never wanted you to . . .

MARY.   I had found honour and decency and comradeship and you destroyed them for me, like a bad child. Why did you do this to me?

EARLE.   I tell you I never wanted . . .

MARY.   I served you faithfully because you were my comrade. I even put courage into you—or what looked like courage. . . .

EARLE.   My God, I can't understand it.

MARY.   Understand what?

EARLE.   How you ever passed for anything but a woman.

MARY.   What do you mean?

EARLE.   You gave me courage? You robbed me of the courage to do what was right and what I believe in, for the courage of a mad animal in a corner.

MARY.   You liar, I tried to make you play the man.

EARLE.   A woman's man. A woman's idea of a man. A swaggering slave.

MARY.   Ned, all I ask is common loyalty.

EARLE.   Where we split, my dear, is on that word "loyalty." You mean a blind obedience to your will!

MARY.   Blind obedience! You could only be loyal and faithful to me when you were lying like a bandaged corpse. . . .

EARLE.   And you were watching me day and night, I know. Day and night. Day and night. Day and

[59]

night.   Like the great mother of the world, till every turn of the bandage round my head seemed to strangle me and bind me to you.   Till the very ticking of the damned clock in the room hammered "*prison*," "*prison*" "*prison*" into my brain.

MARY.   I am glad of only one thing.   That we never came together as husband and wife.   You couldn't wait even for that.   What can I do now ?   I knew once what to do.   You spoilt all that.   I'm neither man nor woman.   I came back to find my mother and ask her to teach me to walk humbly in the way in which it has pleased God to call me.   He is easily pleased.

EARLE.   But not so easily satisfied.   Your story isn't finished.

MARY.   You have no more part in it.

EARLE.   That we cannot tell.   I have been steadfast in one thing.

MARY.   What ?

EARLE.   I am still the man with whom you fell in love.

MARY (*long pause*).   Yes !

[*The* ANABAPTIST *slowly rises.   Staggers over* R. *against the counter, dazed, gazing vacantly.*]

ANABAPTIST (*unseeingly*).   The Lord thy God is a jealous God.   At Tyburn Fields to-day I saw a mighty angel clothed in a cloud.

EARLE.   Who *are* you ?

ANA. (*still unseeing*).   I saw a fool who denied his God choked on the gibbet.

MARY.   He's mad.

ANA. (*gazes round, then fixes his eyes on* MARY).   I'm not mad.   I know what I'm saying.   (*To* EARLE.)   The man on the gibbet was my son.

MARY.   Oh . . .

ANA.   Vengeance.   Vengeance is mine.   I will repay, saith the Lord.

EARLE (*crosses to* ANA.). How dare you speak to that woman, you wicked liar? You maniac.

ANA. I speak with the voice of the Lord of Hosts. (*With a cunning look at* MARY.) I heard what they said of you. They thought I was asleep. They were wrong. He that keepeth Israel shall neither slumber nor sleep. Woman, you have done an abomination in the sight of the Lord. Male and female created he them.

MARY. What do you mean?

ANA. Hide yourself. Hide yourself in the rocky places. Hide in the midst of the ocean, he will find you out.

EARLE. Get out of here. Don't listen to him. Go and rant in the streets, man, and let us alone.

ANA. I will publish it in the streets—yea, I will cry that it shall be done to you as it was done to Oholah and Oholibah, for your frowardness and your lewdness—(*he is now going up the steps*)—to Oholah and Oholibah . . .

[*His voice dies away up the street.*]

MARY. What does he mean? That I am to be punished for what I have done?

EARLE (*laughing wildly*). Yes. Hearken to Israel. Behold the messenger of the Lord. Behold the angel of the Lord.

MARY. Stop that. What's the matter with the whole world? I come back to find this den, and my mother a full-blown harlot, and you a lunatic, Ned Earle.

EARLE. Ah, but the peace, the ineffable, unutterable peace of being mad.

[MARY *picks up cloak and puts it on.*]

You are going?

MARY. Yes. I'll leave you to your peace. If the whole world is against me, if my nature's against me, and this man says God is against me, I'll defy all three.

EARLE. Where are you going?

[61]

MARY. I don't know. To sea, I think, to Pernambuco. (*She laughs.*) Will you come with me?

EARLE. No, by Heaven, no. You've killed my soul, but my body at least is my own. Leave me in my gutter. Never again will you drag me through the hurricane.

MARY. Good-bye then, Ned.

[*She goes.*]

EARLE. Good-bye. Good-bye.

[*He laughs madly.* MRS. READ *enters and joins in.*]

MRS. READ. I thought I heard a noise. This is a very noisy locality, sir. Mr. Spanner is a little indisposed. You were a little—harsh—with him, sir. A little harsh. But . . . where is Mary? Where's that girl?

EARLE (*still laughing a little*). Mother, you have lost your daughter again. You should take more heed to the child.

MRS. READ. Oh, the heartless baggage. Oh, the cruel unfeeling wretch. We must stop her. In what direction did she go?

EARLE. In the direction of Pernambuco, I think. It's the port of Brazil, Mrs. Read. It has a bridge of twenty-eight arches. (MRS. READ *staggers up the stairs outside calling "Mary," "Mary, come back," etc.*) Shout to the West, Mrs. Read. Shout to the West.

CURTAIN

ACT III

SCENE I

SCENE.—*The Governor's quarters in the Fort of the Island of Providence in the Bahamas. It is an evening early in August in the year* 1720.

Some sort of entertainment is in progress behind a curtain at the back of the stage. SPENLOVE *the Governor's Secretary, a tall, dried, yellow young man, is writing at a desk.* EARLE *comes in through the curtain dragging a young lady by the wrist. Neither of them notices* SPENLOVE.

LADY. Don't! You're hurting me.

EARLE. I am cruel, sweetheart, only to be kind.

LADY. It is not kind to make me a laughing-stock. The people will talk (*looking over shoulder*).

EARLE. His Excellency the Governor's guests will talk.

LADY. Yes.

EARLE. I do not doubt it. Talk and talk and talk. They have been talking for an eternity. And what talk! Come, kiss me. (*She kisses him.*) Now is not that a sovran anodyne? It calms the spirit. Once again. . . . It even uplifts the mind. And Heaven knows that is necessary enough in the Bahamas. . . .

LADY. Have you no good word to say of the Bahamas.

EARLE. I like their sunsets. And to-night's above all others. Kiss me again.

LADY. No. You know you . . .

EARLE. Why not?

LADY. I think you are a sad fellow. What must you think of me?

[63]

EARLE.   I think you are an exquisitely formed piece of stupidity, but you have an idea of the principles of at least one civilised custom.   Kiss me again.

LADY.   I shouldn't.

EARLE.   Damn you, Madam, you know neither how to behave nor how to misbehave.   You weary me.

[SPENLOVE *rises*.]

EARLE.   Ah, Spenlove!   I had not observed you, Spenlove.

SPENLOVE.   I conjectured as much, Mr. Earle. . . . Do you wish to remain here, Madam, or shall I conduct you to your husband ?

LADY.   We shouldn't be here at all, Mr. Earle.   This is his Excellency's own room.   Permit me.   I'll retire.

[*She does so in some confusion.*]

EARLE.   Mr. Spenlove, you have added the final abomination to my quite intolerable visit to the Indies.

[EARLE *makes a deprecating gesture.*]

SPENLOVE.   Have you no good word to say of the Bahamas ?

EARLE.   I like their sunsets.   Mr. Spenlove, you must forgive a poodle for being ill at ease among sea-dogs.

SPENLOVE.   Readily, sir.   But you do yourself and us an injustice.   I have heard that you are skilled in navigation.   And you would find us not unhandy at a compliment, if our ears were not continually strained to hear cannon fire, and our eyes to behold the Jolly Roger. You must consider the state of the islands.

EARLE.   I do.   I do.   Say no more about it.   Forgive me; I am a hag-ridden, spell-bound, devil possessed, world-wandering fool.

SPENLOVE.   You malign yourself, sir.

EARLE.   The only things that keeps me standing on my two legs are hatred and contempt for mankind.

[64]

SPENLOVE.   And womankind ?

EARLE.   What the devil do you mean ?

SPENLOVE.   I mean no offence, but your state of mind seemed to be familiar.

EARLE.   Mr. Spenlove, there is nothing in your footman's philosophy that can take account of my complaint.

SPENLOVE.   Sir, you are very flattering.   And now I beg you to excuse me. . . . Well, Trumpet ?

[TRUMPET *enters* L.]

TRUMPET.   Well, Mr. Spenlove ?

SPENLOVE.   His Excellency wishes to see you, Trumpet. I'll tell him you are here.

[SPENLOVE *goes* R.]

EARLE.   Pray excuse me, sir.   What did you say your name was ?

TRUMPET.   John Trumpet, sir.   A trader in these parts.

EARLE.   You have a sweet name, Mr. Trumpet.

TRUMPET.   I am glad that it pleases you, sir.

EARLE.   It pleases me very much indeed.

[SPENLOVE *holds curtain for* ROGERS, R.]

[*Enter* MR. WOODES-ROGERS, R., *a Governor of Providence ; a hearty weather-beaten soul of about fifty.*]

ROGERS.   Ha, Mr. Earle !   Gossiping with Trumpet ? An insult to our local beauties.   I must see to that. Well, you dirty ruffian, what lies have you brought me to-night ?

TRUMPET.   Oh, your Excellency . . .

ROGERS.   We have to use filthy weapons, Mr. Earle, and Trumpet is the filthiest we have ever used.   A vile dog.   A vile dog.   What's this, Speny ?

SPENLOVE.   The new proclamation, your Excellency. I have prepared a more graceful version of that sent by Sir Nicholas and it is ready for your signature.

F   [65]

ROGERS. You will note, Mr. Earle, that I am set here in the midst of a nest of cut-throats and expected to subdue them by proclamations. This island is packed to the foreshore with pirates, waiting till I drop an eyelid to disembowel me and every honest man-jack in the fort. If you take the trip to Pernambuco you propose, Mr. Earle, you're as like as not to be snapped up under my very nose by Bart Roberts or . . .

TRUMPET. Captain John Rackham is operating in these parts.

ROGERS. Calico Jack?

TRUMPET. Yes, sir!

ROGERS. The devil he is. I'll have the pleasure of hanging Master Jack up to dry one of these days. What's the news of Calico Jack?

SPENLOVE. Since he stole Bonny's wife, he's been confining himself to fishing smacks and turtlers and small deer generally.

ROGERS. I had heard that the rogue had become domesticated.

TRUMPET. Not entirely, your Excellency.

ROGERS. I wish you had met Mistress Bonny, Mr. Earle. She has danced here often. A bundle of flaming sin is Mistress Bonny. A bundle of flaming sin. You must stay a little longer and become acquainted with our island society, Mr. Earle. I think . . .

SPENLOVE. If your Excellency pleases, perhaps we had better hear this scoundrel's story and send him packing. It is getting late.

ROGERS. That's right. Speak up, you dirty cur. Are we to dance attendance on you all night? Eh?

TRUMPET. It is about Rackham I had brought you news, your Excellency. He has gathered a fair-sized crew, and is flying at higher game than turtlers—with all respect to you, Mr. Spenlove.

SPENLOVE. This can hardly be of interest to Mr. Earle.

EARLE. You think not?

ROGERS. Of course it is. Get the chart, Spenny. Come along, Mr. Earle, you shall help to catch Calico Jack. Ah, there now. Where did you sight the brute last, you hound?

TRUMPET. He is bound for Cuba. But I have arranged a friendly rendezvous with him for the end of the month on Cat Island. At Pont Negril on Cat Island on the twenty-seventh of the month.

ROGERS. Then we must send a frigate. What's your business with Calico Jack?

TRUMPET. It's rather a delicate matter, sir.

SPENLOVE. We've always found it injudicious to be too particular as to Mr. Trumpet's business.

ROGERS. Pont Negril you say, Cat Island?

TRUMPET. On the twenty-seventh.

ROGERS. If we could believe a word you say, you filthy villain.

TRUMPET. Oh, your Excellency.

ROGERS. We haven't a stool pigeon to join Rackham's pirates, and keep us in touch with their movements, hey?

TRUMPET. We had one, your Excellency.

ROGERS. How d'ye mean, had?

TRUMPET. Alas, he met with an accident, poor young fellow.

ROGERS. Now who could we send? Who could we send?

SPENLOVE. There isn't a soul we could trust, sir.

EARLE. Would you care to trust me?

ROGERS. You, Mr. Earle?

SPENLOVE. I hardly think . . .

EARLE. Yes. I have a mind to try your Calico Jacks and your Ann Bonnys. If you will guarantee me against a judicial hanging I should like to be a spy.

SPENLOVE. But you're a sick man.

ROGERS. But look you, my boy, you're risking your life. . . .

EARLE. I have a good record as an officer in the Navy, sir. In the Army my record was not so good.

ROGERS. You haven't the cut of a fighting man.

EARLE. I have this fighting quality, that I cannot bear the stigma of defeat.

ROGERS. Defeat? I cannot recollect that our Navy . . .

EARLE. My own defeat. I have an ignominy to blot out. I am determined to serve you, sir.

SPENLOVE. We cannot allow . . .

TRUMPET. If his Excellency will pardon me, perhaps you will let me tell you, sir, the nature of the unpleasant accident that befell your predecessor. A mulatto, a charming young fellow.

ROGERS. What happened to him?

TRUMPET. Will Read, the soldier, caught him signalling with a storm lamp to the mainland.

ROGERS. Well, and then . . .

SPENLOVE. What did he do?

TRUMPET. He cut him into gobbets where he stood.

EARLE. What name did you say?

TRUMPET. The mulatto, sir?

EARLE. No, the other, the soldier.

TRUMPET. Will Read. They call him the Soldier because he fought in Flanders. The pirates recruited him last year. He seems to be the life of the venture. An ambitious young fellow, a dangerous fellow.

EARLE. So it comes out. It was settled before I was born.

ROGERS. I beg your pardon, Mr. Earle.

EARLE. Captain Rogers, I am at your service. I feel sure that the Soldier and I will be great friends.

CURTAIN

[68]

ACT III

SCENE II

The after cabin of the " Mallard." Music from the Orchestra rises to a crescendo and there is heard above it the sound of firing off stage L. The curtain rises quickly, showing a Master and two sailors barricading a door in the half-light. They are utilising two large chests. Suddenly there is a lull in the noise.

1ST SAILOR.   My soul.   They're quiet all of a sudden. What are they doin' ?

2ND SAILOR.   Cuttin' throats like sheep in a slaughter-house.

MASTER.   Hold your tongue, MacGregor.

VOICE.   Open the door there.

1ST SAILOR.   This is one bit o' the ship yon pirate scum won't get.

[*He fires a pistol through the door.*]

MASTER.   Reload, you.

2ND SAILOR.   What's the good ?   They've took the ship.   It's their ship now.

MASTER.   It's my ship while I'm standing in a square foot of it.   She's no prize for a gang o' pirates while I'm still alive.

VOICE (*outside*).   Keep back from them doors.   They're in there.

ANOTHER.   Hi there, Mister.   Come out o' that.

MASTER.   Come in an' fetch us an' be damned to you.

VOICE.   This way, Quartermaster.   It's the Master and two or three others.   I saw them go in.

CORNER.   You did ?   Come out, rot you.   The game's up.

[69]

MARY.   What's amiss in there?

CORNER.   Look out, Soldier. They've got pistols.

MARY.   Stand clear all.

[*Maroon and flash.*]

[*There is a blinding explosion. The door caves in. One of the chests falls to bits, revealing that it has been full of clothing. Pirates rush in, led by* MARY. *She cuts down a sailor.*]

SAILOR.   Quarter, Soldier, quarter.

MARY.   Who told you Rackham's men gave quarter? Bring in the lanterns there.

[*Pirates enter with lanterns.*]

SAILOR.   I'm a poor honest man, sir. Spare me; I'll do anything. Spare me. I've a wife and six children.

MARY.   It would be a pity to rob your wife of a man like you. Lift these two up. They're not dead. The surgeon 'd better see them.

CORNER.   You hear what the Soldier says. Lay off that chest. You and the rest of you, take your bug-bitten bodies out o' this.

HARWOOD.   It's all right, Dick Corner. We're doing all the work.

CORNER.   You tin-eyed worm. Don't you talk to me, see.

HARWOOD.   Fair   word,   Quartermaster.   We're gentlemen adventurers like yourself.

CORNER.   If you want trouble, it's here and ready for you, see. Yes, and for the rest of you. Look lively.

[*Pirates and prisoners have all gone by this.*]

Hijos di puta. (*Sees* MARY *tying up her wrist.*) Hurt yourself, Will?

MARY.   It's nothing.

CORNER.   You ought to take things quieter.

MARY.   How's that?

CORNER. Aw, forget you was a soldier, see. Take it easy, sailor fashion, same as we do.

MARY. Hah! Sailor fashion? You're a good sailor anyway.

CORNER. Pretty good, Will. Pretty . . .

MARY. How many points were you out in your reckoning this passage?

CORNER. Heh?

MARY. It was plain luck you kept us off the reef out there, and you know it.

CORNER. Now see here, Will Read. I don't set up for being no ruddy navigator. That's book larnin'. But I can fudge a day's work. And though you're a mate of mine, I can fight as well as any soldier. Keep a mind o' that.

[*Goes to door* L.]

MARY (*looking off*). Jack Davis, here!

DAVIS (*entering*). Here, Soldier.

MARY. Go to the Master Gunner and tell him to get around at once and uncloy any of the guns they've had the sense to spike.

CORNER (*looking off door* L.). Strike me poxy, here's old John Trumpet just come aboard from the long-boat.

MARY. And tell Mr. Featherstone, if the Captain hasn't mounted a guard on the rum barrel, he'd better do it himself. Peralta and Boult tell him. That's all. Look alive.

DAVIS. Aye, aye, Soldier.

CORNER. There's Jack Rackham and Ann Bonny, curse me, welcoming the old fox aboard like a bloody levee.

MARY. What old fox?

CORNER. John Trumpet, I'm tellin' yer. He's lost no time coming off from his pickings. Out of every shilling of prize-money that comes to us, he'll have half mebbe. The lousy kite.

MARY. It's a pity we can't be honest rogues without the stink of a fence hanging over all.

[71]

CORNER. Rot me, Will. God made the world the way it would work.

RACKHAM (*entering*). This way, Mr. Trumpet. This way. Ah, all snug an' shipshape. And as tidy forrard, begad. Annie! Fetch in that bill-of-lading. Well, Soldier, what d'ye think o' the prize? A trim ship, Mr. Featherstone, eh?

[ANN *enters, crosses to* RACKHAM, *sitting on chest.*]

FEATHERSTONE. A trimmer ship than the old one yonder.

RACKHAM. Outsail her, you reckon?

FEATHERSTONE. Ay, she'd lie a point closer maybe.

ANN. Then, oddslife, we'll ship on her and send the old brig to the bottom.

RACKHAM. Good thought, my darling. That'll cover our tracks and give a clean pair of heels to show the King's frigates, rot 'em. And now, Mr. Trumpet, to business. I suppose you're here to cheat us out of our prize, ransoms an' all.

TRUMPET. Now, now, now, Captain. Come, come, come. I'm an honest trader.

RACKHAM. Then I'm a rosy-cheeked choir-boy. Well, here's the cargo. When do we get the money? Come, speak up.

TRUMPET. You're always in such a hurry, Captain.

RACKHAM. D'ye think we're here to wait for your convenience? There's a packet of ransoms you owe us still from our last piece of business. What of that?

TRUMPET. The rendezvous for the payment of that is fixed, Captain, don't you remember? Pont Negril, Cat Island, on the twenty-seventh of the month.

RACKHAM. So be it. But no trickery, mind, or . . . By the way, who's that you've brought off with you on the boat? Another honest trader, eh?

TRUMPET. He's a—a refugee from the plantations.

[72]

RACKHAM.   If you're trying to plant another dirty spy on us . . .

TRUMPET.   Captain Rackham, on my honour.   This man's my wife's cousin.   A gentleman born.

RACKHAM.   What was he transported for ?

TRUMPET.   For . . . murder.   But a most genteel and creditable murder.

RACKHAM.   What should I be doing with your lousy murderers ?

TRUMPET.   He's an expert navigator.

RACKHAM.   A sea-artist eh ?

TRUMPET.   Yes.   Was in the Navy.

RACKHAM (*moving* L. *to look at chest*).   We could be doing with a sea-artist.

MARY.   We could.

ANN.   And that's the truth.

FEATHERSTONE.   Mr. Trumpet!

[TRUMPET *joins* FEATHERSTONE *and* RACKHAM.]

CORNER.   Will Read!   Come now, Will.

MARY.   What's the matter with you, Dick Corner ? You don't set up as a navigator.

CORNER.   No, but I got you here, didn't I ?

MARY.   It was luck that got us here.

CORNER.   And seamanship.   You don't . . .

RACKHAM.   Belay there!   You're a damn bad navigator, Dick, and you know it.

CORNER.   And you'd turn me away for some counter-jumping swab, planted on you by the likes of that ?

RACKHAM.   I would.

MARY.   If he can con the ship he's worth the risk. Don't be a fool.

CORNER.   A fool, am I ?

ANN.   Everyone knows that.

CORNER.   Well, he can con you to hell for all I care. But when you're swinging sun-dried at the end of a rope . . .

[73]

RACKHAM. Dick Corner, you dirty swab, do you threaten me?

MARY. Quit hazing, Captain.

CORNER. No, but I warn you . . .

RACKHAM. Oh, stow your gab. I'm captain of this ship.

MARY. And lucky to be that. Where were you at the boarding?

RACKHAM. Holy sailor!

MARY. Ann Bonny and I took the ship while you were skulking.

RACKHAM. By thunder! I'll teach you who's captain of this ship. I'll take what I want and keep what I want, and answer no God-damned son of a monkey what I do. And now, Mr. John Trumpet, we'll see to the prisoners and the stores in the hold, for the sooner the ship's clear of you the better I'll be pleased; eh, Annie? And as for that damned sea-artist of yours, I'll take him; we'll watch him like a cat at a mouse-hole. And if he's a spy I'll cut the hearts out of both of you. Come on. Corner, Featherstone, follow me.

[ANN *opens chest and pulls out some lady's clothing. She begins to undress, not seeing* MARY. *The garments awaken* MARY'S *interest.* ANN *suddenly discovers* MARY.]

ANN. In the name of the holy Saints!

MARY. I beg your pardon. I didn't notice how you were.

ANN. You didn't notice. You must be a curious sort of young man.

MARY. Do you think so? (*Pause.*) China silk! (*to herself*).

ANN. Will, Will, do you like me?

MARY. Yes.

ANN. Then you're mighty insensible to your privileges.

MARY.   What privileges?

ANN.   Most gentleman adventurers who have seen what you have seen would have forgotten all about Jack Rackham by this time.

MARY.   Huh! (*laughing*).   I've seen a woman in her shift before.

ANN.   I'm sure of that.   But it's a sight that never seems to pall on the gentlemen.   No? . . . Either you don't like me or you're afraid of Jack Rackham.   Which is it?

MARY.   I like you, Ann, and I'm not afraid of God, man or devil.

ANN.   Kiss me then.

MARY.   That's a favour I like to ask for myself.

ANN.   Ask it then.   You're killing me, Will.   You're so young and brave and gentle.   You don't stink of tar and tobacco and rumbo like that filthy old pirate. You've got a soft voice and soft hands.   (*Begins to paw* MARY.)

MARY.   That's great foolishness, Ann.

ANN.   Why is it?   You don't know what love means. I'll teach you.

MARY.   I know what love means.   Better than you do perhaps.

ANN.   You don't, you don't.   Why do you kill me, Will?   I know you think me a common trull.

MARY.   No, you're a heart of gold, and a good comrade, and a little beauty too.   I love you in my way, but it's not the way you think.

ANN.   What way is that?   It is no way at all.   If you love me in any way, why don't you take me, and to hell with Jack Rackham?

MARY.   Because I'm a woman.   [ANN *laughs.*]

Yes.   I'm a woman like yourself.   (*She rises.*)

ANN.   Madre di dios!   Is that true?

MARY.   Yes.   Hold up, Ann.

ANN. Holy Saints. It's like a nightmare.

MARY. I can't think why I told you. Only a feeling came over me that I'd like someone to know.

ANN. I must wake up. I must wake up.

MARY. You'll speak of this to no one, or I'll choke the life out of you.

ANN. I will not. Tell me, why did you do it? Why did you turn soldier and pirate and all?

MARY. I like rough devils better than smooth ones.

ANN. That's what I say. Hell for company. I had my fill of fine gentlemen in the sugar plantations, with their "Pray Ma'ams" and their "Oh Ma'ams," and their "Madam, your obedients." They can't ask a girl for what they want without simpering and play-acting. And then along came Calico Jack like a great roaring stallion. I thought I'd died and gone to heaven.

MARY. I thought you liked me for my daintiness and genteel ways?

ANN. Och, that's another bit o' my notion of heaven. Variety.

MARY. You've a strange idea of heaven. Do you like being pawed and leered at and lied to?

ANN. Why, yes, I do. But I like to stand away from it sometimes.

MARY. I like to stand away from it always.

ANN. You should have been a nun.

MARY. Oh, prisons, prisons, prisons. I'll be dead soon enough and crushed down narrowly by the earth or the green seas.

ANN. Och, we'll all be dead and gone to heaven soon, so what does it matter? Let's make ourselves handsome. I thought I should try this one first.

MARY. I'll help you, you black-faced trollop. Hold your breath.

[RACKHAM *enters.*]

RACKHAM. What's this?

ANN. Jack, no.   It's a mistake.

[RACKHAM *knocks* MARY *down and draws knife.* ANN
    struggles with him.]

RACKHAM.   A mistake.   By thunder, you'll find it's
a mistake, you slut.   I'll teach you to make a cuckold of
Jack Rackham.   I'll cut your back to ribbons with the tail
end of a rope, but I'll have the liver out of this cock first.

ANN (*still struggling*).   No, Jack, no.   Help! Help!

[CORNER *rushes on.*]

CORNER.   What's all this ?

ANN.   It's murder.   Don't let him, Dick.   Don't let
him.   It's a mistake.   It's all a mistake.

CORNER.   What's the trouble, Captain ?

RACKHAM.   Get out of my way, Corner, or you'll get
it too.

CORNER.   No, no.   Captain.   Free companions' law.
You can't fight a messmate aboard ship.

RACKHAM.   Fight ?   Who said fight ?   There'll be
no fight.

[RACKHAM *draws pistol.   As he fires,* CORNER *knocks it up.*]

What's this, you mutinous hound ?

CORNER.   Fair words, Captain.

RACKHAM.   Call the men aft.   Do you hear me ?
Pipe the men aft.   I'll show my pretty Soldier he can't
make a cuckold of Jack Rackham.

[CORNER *makes no move.*]

Am I captain of this ship ?

CORNER.   You are, sir, but you can't get beyond
pirates' law.   You must fight it out ashore.

[*He helps* MARY *to her feet.*]

Come, Will.

MARY.   Thank you, Dick Corner.   I'll not forget it.

[CORNER *and* MARY *go.*]

[77]

RACKHAM. And as for you, Mistress, this afternoon Sambo the black 'll give you the Law of Moses on the bare back for all the crew to see. And to-morrow the landcrabs 'll pick your parmour's ribs.

ANN. Will they? (*Laughs.*) Oh, Jack, win or lose, you'll furnish many a laugh to your seamen and their Delilahs in the days to come. The little black boys will be singing bawdy ballads of you.

RACKHAM. What are you at, you jade?

ANN. Poor old Jack, ask Will Read to take off his shirt.

RACKHAM. Why?

ANN. Will Read's a girl.

RACKHAM. Holy sailor!

ANN. How do you like that, Jack?

RACKHAM. Like it? I feel like a round shot in the guts.

ANN. Well, well, come forrard and float it off in Rumbo.

RACKHAM. Rum, that's it. Rum.

[TRUMPET *is heard showing in* EARLE.]

TRUMPET (*entering*). Come along, Mr. Earle. Oh, Captain Rackham, this is Mr. Earle. Mr. Earle, this is Captain John Rackham.

EARLE. I am honoured to meet so celebrated a person. I have often heard, etc., etc.

TRUMPET. This is the gentleman I told you about, etc., etc.

RACKHAM. Rot that, you chattering bastards. We've had all that. He's a murderer and a sea-artist. Want to ship with us, cock?

EARLE. I intend that.

RACKHAM. Very well then. I like the looks of you, but I don't like your friends. I'll have my eye on you like a cat at a mouse-hole. I'll have you watched night and day.

[78]

EARLE.   You honour me, sir.

RACKHAM.   Your servant, sir, and you can see the Quartermaster about where you're to heave your dunny-bag.   Blood and wounds, is this the Arabian desert? Where's that drink, Featherstone?   We must drink to our next merry meeting.   Pont Negril, eh?

TRUMPET.   On the 27th.

RACKHAM.   And you've to get us there, eh, Mr. Navigator?

EARLE.   I'll get you there.

RACKHAM.   Come along then.   If the rum won't come to us, we'll dive into the rum.

> [RACKHAM *goes.* TRUMPET *and* ANN *also make to go. As* EARLE *moves,* TRUMPET *stops him with a* "*Hist.*" ANN *stops, senses the by-play and then bows mockingly to both,* TRUMPET *saying,* "*After you, Mrs. Bonny.*" ANN *then goes.* TRUMPET *crosses to* EARLE L., *at door.*]

TRUMPET.   Pont Negril, Cat Island.

> [TRUMPET *exits, meeting* MARY *just outside.*]

MARY (*enters*).   It's you, Ned.

EARLE.   Yes.

MARY.   You've come at last.

EARLE.   Yes.

MARY.   I knew you'd come.   I'm glad to see you, Ned.

CURTAIN

ACT III

SCENE III

The deck of the " Mallard," which has recently come to anchor at Pont Negril, Cat Island. Members of the crew are engaged in various jobs, splicing ropes, coiling cables and hawsers, whilst others are dicing, etc., and some are even dozing on the deck. Musician is playing, etc.

FEATHERSTONE is supervising the work whilst CORNER is sitting moodily on a keg smoking and obviously sulking.

Within the fore-cabin RACKHAM's voice is heard and evidently the worse of drink.

RACKHAM (*within*). Send in that fiddler; and what's the matter with the grog?

FRENCHMAN (*who is coming forward carrying a large steaming bowl*). Coming, sir, coming.

NEGRO (*following him with a steaming bucket*). Coming, sah!

HARWOOD. What's that you've got, doctor?

FEATHERSTONE. Don't stop him. Calico Jack's serving hot burnt brandy to all hands.

DAVIS. What for?

FEATHERSTONE. A record voyage.

HARWOOD. The sea-artist. He done that.

DAVIS. A day ahead of time, man.

CORNER (*spitting in disgust*). The sea-artist.

[*The men begin to file into the cabin.*]

A PIRATE. Whoever done it, I'm for a smell of the hot grog.

ANOTHER. What's that, grog?

ANOTHER. A bloody tay-party.

[80]

ANOTHER.   Come along, boys, to the tay-party.

DAVIS (*going off says something to* FEATHERSTONE).

FEATHERSTONE.   The Captain to you, my lad.   Neat and handy there.   Work first, play after.

DAVIS.   Aye, aye, Featherstone, damn your eyes. Half of them's in already, look you.

[*Going in,* FEATHERSTONE *makes a blow at him.*]

FEATHERSTONE.   Coming, Dick?

CORNER.   No.

RACKHAM (*entering*).   Where's Dick Corner?

FEATHERSTONE.   Says he won't come, Captain.

RACKHAM.   Says he?   The broken-backed muck-worm. . . . Come along, Dick Corner, get under way.

CORNER.   Never mind about me.   Go to your tay-party.

RACKHAM.   Why, we need you at the tay-party. Come along.

CORNER.   No.

RACKHAM.   Wazzermazzer with you?   Why not?

CORNER.   I don't feel like it, that's all.

RACKHAM.   But it's cerrebellation, Dick.   A party. This is the rendezvous, ain't it?

CORNER.   Aye!

RACKHAM.   Pont Negril on Cat Island, ain't it?

CORNER.   That's right.

RACKHAM.   The twenty-sixth, ain't it?

CORNER.   Yes.

RACKHAM.   Very well then.   We're in twenty-four hours ahead of time.   And all thanks to our noble navigating Lieutenant, God bless him.

CORNER.   Your noble navigator . . . a crucified spy, that's what he is.

RACKHAM.   What's that you say?

CORNER.   That swab's a spy.   A red stinking stool-pigeon.

RACKHAM.   No, no, Dick.   Fair words now, Dick.

G   [81]

CORNER. He's a spy, I tell you And I'll tell him so too and ram it down his bloody throat.

RACKHAM. Now, now, now, Dick. Hold hard there, Dick. A happy ship. That's not conviviality, Dick, all friends and good shipmates on this ship. It's a happy ship, Dick. Isn't it a happy ship, Misser Featherstone?

FEATHERSTONE (*sadly*). Aye, aye. It's a happy ship.

RACKHAM. There, what'd I tell you? Very well, then. Come along and kiss the sea-artist.

CORNER. I'll see him in hell first.

RACKHAM (*louder*). Are you going to obey my orders, you swab?

ANN. Oh, rot that, Jack, the boys are waiting for you. Take his other arm, Featherstone. You'd better come, Dick.

CORNER (*going*). I know damn well he's a spy.

[FEATHERSTONE *pilots the grumbling* RACKHAM *out.*]

[EARLE *is up on poop deck.* MARY *enters. When he hears her step he spins round abruptly. He registers some relief when he sees who it is.*]

EARLE. Ah, Mr. Read.   (*Comes down ladder to deck.*)

MARY. Well?

EARLE. Wait. I want to speak to you.

MARY. I'll wait.

[EARLE *comes down to the deck.*]

MARY. What do you want?

EARLE. Mary, I've been on this damned boat for a day and a night, and this is the first opportunity . . .

MARY. Do you know why I'm speaking to you now? Why I'm here now?

EARLE. No doubt you have some reason.

MARY. Because it is my watch.

EARLE. What's that? What do you mean?

MARY. Surely you know that you are being watched?

[82]

You have never been out of sight since you came on board.

EARLE. I know that. This butcher's tub is full of eyes. If it hadn't been for you I'd have hit Jack Rackham on the jaw and gone to Davy Jones like a gentleman. Why are they watching me?

MARY. They think you are a spy.

EARLE. Do they? Do you?

MARY. I hope that you are not.

EARLE. It would be unlike me to take that risk, you think?

MARY. Yes, but you have changed.

EARLE. Yes, I have changed. I thought I was the kind of man who could stand apart and watch the world as if it were a show. You dragged me down from my place and broke me on the rocks. I am glad you did.

MARY. Glad?

EARLE. Yes. I have no more to fear now.

MARY. Are you a spy?

EARLE. What if I were?

MARY. I don't know. If I weren't a woman I'd know what to do. Tell me the truth, Ned. Only this once.

EARLE. I am the Governor's agent. A spy if you like. And now what will you do with me?

MARY (under her breath). God has played a trick on me.

EARLE (sotto voce but passionately). Mary, let us make an end of all this. Come away from here. Come out of this riot of brute beasts. Our life's beginning now. (Embrace.) We have the chance. We'll take the pink and make for the shore. I know . . . the chart shows. . . . There's a hiding-place on the windward beach. A cave. . . . We could lie safe there . . . until . . . we could lie safe there for to-day and to-night.

MARY. And then, after I'd betrayed my comrades? After we'd lain safe for a day and a night, what then?

G 2   [83]

EARLE.   Leave that to me.   I can get you away.

MARY.   Have you and Trumpet set a trap for to-morrow ?

EARLE.   Yes.

MARY.   What sort of a trap ?

EARLE.   I was to signal.

MARY.   How ?

EARLE.   With a red flare to the shore.

MARY.   To a spy on shore ?

EARLE.   Yes.

MARY.   What would happen then ?

EARLE.   Nothing will happen.   I shall give no signal.

MARY.   Then you are betraying the Governor too ?

EARLE.   What is the Governor to me or your murdering pirates to you ?   We're Mary Read and Ned Earle. We've found ourselves, don't you understand ?   We've no art or part in this chicanery and murder.   Come. Come now.

[*Cabin door* P.S. *opens.   Noise of rowdy crew.*]

MARY.   Careful !

[ANN BONNY *enters.*   EARLE *dodges behind* R. *of mast.*]

Well, Ann ?

ANN.   Well.   You're having a pleasant talk with our sea-artist, are you ?

MARY.   Why, yes !

ANN (*mimicking her*).   Why, yes !   Congratulating him on the passage ?

MARY.   It was a good passage.

ANN.   And a lovely subject for a conversation. You're mighty great friends with the sea-artist all of a sudden.

MARY.   Don't be foolish.

ANN.   Foolish ?   You'd better go into the foc's'le and hear what the men have to say about your noble navigating lieutenant.

[84]

EARLE (*coming forward*). Why don't they say it to me?

ANN. They'll say it to you all right, and if you don't want to get the Soldier into trouble . . .

MARY. That's not like you, Ann Bonny.

ANN. It's like me to say what I mean. What made you sneak away from the men just now? Not good enough for you, are we?

EARLE. What's the matter with you?

ANN. The matter with you is that Dick Corner's out for your blood. And he's in the right of it too, as you'll find, Soldier, before you're much older.

[*Suddenly the* O.P. *door opens and* CORNER *rushes out followed by* FEATHERSTONE *and a bunch of pirates.*]

CORNER. I'll show you. I'll settle the dirty stool-pigeon.

FEATHERSTONE. Come back, Dick. You're spoiling the party. Handsome and easy, Dick.

[RACKHAM *enters the* P.S. *door roaring drunk.*]

RACKHAM. Dick Corner or no Dick Corner, he's crossed me, d'ye hear? I'll cut the guts out of Dick Corner. Annie, he's spoilt the celebrations.

ANN (*holding him back*). Easy, Jack, easy.

[*They get* RACKHAM *out again.*]

CORNER. Stand back there, Featherstone.

MARY. What d'ye want, Dick?

CORNER. I want a word with the sea-artist.

MARY. Well, I'm talking to him. You can have your word with him later.

CORNER. I'll have it now. (FEATHERSTONE *tries to restrain him.*) Belay there, Feathers. You listen to this, boys. You don't believe me? I'll show you. . . . You there. (EARLE *is pushed round to face* CORNER.) You was transported to the plantations they say.

[85]

EARLE. Yes.

CORNER. How long have you known Trumpet, hey?

EARLE. We are lifelong friends.

CORNER. Don't jockey me. We know you took the place of that mulatto spy. You'll get what he got.

ANN. Corner, hold your tongue. Can't you see it's his game to make you angry? (*To* EARLE.) Why did Trumpet bring you here?

MARY (*getting between them*). You're a great pair of lawyers, you two, with your cross-questioning. Go away back to the fo'c'sle and get it off your stomach there.

[*General muttering.*]

CORNER. This ain't your affair, Will Read.

MARY. Not my affair, isn't it? Whose watch on the sea-artist is it? Yours or mine? By God I'll show you whose affair it is.

HARWOOD. Fair words, Soldier. If he's not a spy he can speak up for himself.

MARY. Who said he was a spy?

HARWOOD. Dick Corner, he said so.

MARY. And you'll parrot Dick Corner will you, and shove in your mouth in front of your betters? I tell you he's no spy.

CORNER. Who says so?

MARY. I say so!

CORNER. What I want to know . . .

MARY. What I want to know is what the whole pack of you are doing here? I'm doing my duty and I'll thank you to leave me to it.

FEATHERSTONE. Get out of here the lot of you. . . .

[*Pushes the Pirates out.*]

Now, Dick, quit getting these ideas into your head. You never get them out again. The lad's all right. The Soldier says so.

CORNER. I don't take the Soldier's say so.

MARY. You don't, don't you?

FEATHERSTONE. Careful, now.

CORNER. It's all right, Feathers, me and Will ain't going to fight over the likes of that. Get forrard and enjoy yourself. I'll follow you.

FEATHERSTONE. Don't you take any notice of him, Soldier. He's two or three sheets in the wind and a bit ugly.

MARY. He'll have to be a bit uglier before we part hawsers. All right.

ANN. Soldier, it's a trap. Don't you see it's a trap?

MARY. I can look after myself. Don't break your heart about me, Ann Bonny.

ANN. It's not my heart will be broken over this.

[ANN *exits.*]

CORNER (*slowly approaches* EARLE). Who are you?

EARLE. I am well known in other circles than these for a person of fastidious tastes; and apropos of that . . .

CORNER. Don't sling your filthy Dutch at me, d'ye hear?

EARLE. Yes, my man, I hear . . . and I may tell you that your voice, your appearance and the peculiar stench you emit . . .

MARY. Ned, take care . . .

CORNER. What's that you said?

EARLE. You heard me. Your presence makes me sick.

MARY. Dick! Ned! No, no.

CORNER (*hits* EARLE). Do you understand that, you son of a strumpet, or would you like me to spit in your eye?

[MARY *throws* CORNER *right. He nearly falls.*]

EARLE. No, thank you.

CORNER. You know what that means?

EARLE. Yes!

CORNER. Seven o'clock then, to-morrow. Ashore with cutlasses. Featherstone 'll see fair play.

MARY. No, he won't. . . . You saved my life, Dick; we're friends. Will you take a friend's word for Mr. Earle and his apology?

EARLE. Apology! (*Darts forward.*)

CORNER. He's a spy. And he said things to me no man can say and live.

MARY. Dick, I'll stand surety for him.

EARLE. This is my affair.

MARY. Let it alone.

CORNER. Will, I've said I'd fight, and fight I'm going to. You know me, Will Read.

               [CORNER *goes over to R. of mast.*]

MARY. Yes . . . I know you.

EARLE. Let it be.

MARY. *You* can't fight a duel. He'll kill you. He's the best swordsman on the ship.

CORNER. No friend of yours, ain't he?

MARY. What do you mean by that?

CORNER. Why don't you kiss the lousy land-crab?

MARY. Damnation, I'll have a word with you. He isn't the one you've got to fight. By God, no!

EARLE. Take care, it's bad enough as it is.

CORNER. Hold hard, Will.

MARY. Leave this to me, Ned. You drunken bully-ing hound, you'll answer to me, do you hear?

CORNER. I'm your friend, Will.

MARY. Yes, I thought you were once. I know now that you're a fawning lickspittle and a lying Judas Iscariot.

CORNER. Strike me blind, you'll answer for that.

MARY. Yes. I'll answer for it. You'll fight your match with me to-morrow morning.

CORNER. What?

MARY. Are you afraid?

[88]

CORNER. Afraid? It's too dark to fight now, but I'll rip you to bits at sunrise, and the other swab after, strike me blind.

EARLE. This can't be, Corner ; listen to me . . .

MARY. Be quiet, you. Cutlasses and knives?

CORNER. Cutlasses and knives, and the Lord help you.

[*Exit* CORNER R.C.]

EARLE. You'll be killed.

MARY. He was my best friend on the ship.

EARLE. You can't take this fight on you.

MARY. Why not? These fellows are good with a bottle and a black jack, but not one of them can handle a small sword. I'll pink him deep enough to give him a lesson and lay him out for a week or two.

EARLE. No, no. It can't be. I can't let you. . . .

MARY. He won't hurt me. I promise you that. Ned, you won't grudge me my last fling as a fighter? Let me have my way. I'll settle with Dick, and the rest of the crew won't dare to raise a whisper then, except Ann Bonny, and I'll settle with her.

EARLE. No. Such as it is, I'll do my own fighting.

MARY. But, Ned, you'll be killed. He's the best swordsman on the ship.

EARLE. That makes the prospect something pleasanter. I'd hate to have the business botched.

MARY. Hush. Oh, God I love you, Ned.

EARLE. I love you.

MARY. Me? A great murdering brute with a hanging face?

EARLE. You're fine and gallant and gracious. Take me into your greatness and gentleness, my dear one.

MARY. They'll let us be now till to-morrow. Let us have peace for a little.

[*They sit together on the hatch. Song starts.*]

Ned, shall we go to *England*? They have kind

[89]

skies there and the birds are soft and grey, and not like hard, cruel little coloured flames.

[*The men are heard singing in the fo'c'sle.*]

EARLE.   My sister has a house near Tewkesbury, with a garden running down to the Severn.   In the autumn the oaks are the colour of gold.

MARY.   What like is your sister ?

EARLE.   What do you think ?

MARY.   I don't know.

EARLE.   Try to picture her.   Shut your eyes.   Do you see her ?

MARY.   Wait; I think I can.

EARLE.   Then you're wrong.   She is six feet high. She has a voice like a grenadier, a husband like a monkey, and five weakly children.

MARY (*stops a moment to listen to the singing*).   Poor dogs, I'll be sorry to leave them.

[*The song begins to fade out.*]

EARLE.   You'll never be sad or sorry again.

MARY.   And you'll be true to me for ever ?

EARLE.   For ever.

MARY.   Ned, you can do what you like with me, for I'm only a poor weak woman.

CURTAIN

ACT III

SCENE IV

*The same as Scene iii. The morning after Scene iii. It is still
dark, but the first streaks of dawn are coming.* EARLE *is
asleep on deck.* ANN *is up on steps looking through spyglass.*

EARLE (*tenderly*). Mary! where are you? Is that
you, Mary? What are you doing there?

[ANN *comes over* R. *to him. She now holds a pistol.*]

Where is . . . ? What do you want?

ANN. Good morning, spy.

EARLE. Where is . . where's Will Read?

ANN. Will Read! Do you think I'm a fool?

EARLE. Where is she?

ANN. She's where you sent her.

EARLE. Oh, my God! What has happened?

ANN. You've sent her to her death.

EARLE. But she was here, on the deck. She didn't
wake me. I thought . . . is she dead?

ANN. How should I know? Perhaps not yet.

EARLE. But it's daybreak. I must go. I must go
at once. . . .

ANN (*threatening him with a pistol*). Stay where you
are.

EARLE. Mistress Bonny, I am not a particularly
chivalrous man and, to tell you the truth, I am rather
desperate. Have you anything to say to me?

ANN. Yes. The crew think you're a spy. They say
that the first clear sign of it will send you after the mulatto,
among the sharks.

EARLE. Then why didn't they stand to it when I
was face to face with them?

[91]

ANN.   They were face to face with the Soldier.

EARLE.   Wasn't her word good enough for them?

ANN.   It wasn't good enough for me.   I know what she is and what you've done to her.   They don't know she's lying to save her *lover*.   I do.   And I'll do more than that to save *my* lover and *my* ship.

EARLE.   What will you do?

ANN.   She's gone ashore to fight Corner.   I saw them go.   I'll see that she doesn't come back aboard this ship.

EARLE.   But . . . she's your friend.

ANN.   She's protected a spy.   She's betrayed the ship. If you're having our lives, we'll have yours, and your fancy girl's first.

EARLE.   Do you mean that?

ANN.   I do.   She's a dead woman now.

EARLE.   If she's dead, I'm dead too.   There's one thing about a dead man, he's not afraid.   (*Glances over her shoulder.*)   Look behind you, Ann Bonny.

[*As* ANN *turns he leaps at her and throws her on the deck, runs to poop, lights red flare and jumps overboard.*]

ANN (*recovering*).   Peralta!   Harwood!   Davis! Stop him!   He's a spy!   Stop him!

[*A* SAILOR *fires a shot.   To her* RACKHAM.   *He is sober now.   Shouts are heard.   It is nearly daybreak.*]

RACKHAM.   Don't shoot.   After him, you rats.   Take him alive.   (*Men dive.*)   What happened, Annie?   Are you hurt?

ANN.   No, but he half throttled me.

RACKHAM.   Who did?

ANN.   The sea-artist.   He's a spy.   I tell you he's a spy.   He signalled to the creek.

RACKHAM.   Blood and wounds.   (*Runs up companion.*) Where's Will Read?

ANN.   Ashore fighting Corner.

[92]

RACKHAM. Fighting Corner? In God's name why? Why wasn't I told of this? Why wasn't I told?

ANN. You were too drunk, that's why. Keep your head, Jack.

RACKHAM. He signalled the shore?

ANN. Yes.

RACKHAM. Are you certain?

ANN. Yes, yes, yes. With a flare. I saw.

RACKHAM. That means red-coats on the shore and a frigate on the way. I smell death.

ANN. I smell stale rum. Be a man.

RACKHAM. If we up anchor, they'll give chase.

ANN. We can give them a running fight.

RACKHAM. Featherstone! Corner! Harwood!

SAILOR. Here's Featherstone, sir.

[FEATHERSTONE *and* MARY *enter* L.]

RACKHAM. Oh, you're there, Featherstone? Where the hell have you been?

FEATHERSTONE. Ask Will Read. I'm sick in the belly.

RACKHAM. Sick in the belly, was you? You'd back answer me, would you? Am I the captain of this packet or am I not?

ANN. Handsomely, Jack, handsomely.

RACKHAM. What've you been doing?

MARY. I've killed Dick Corner.

RACKHAM. You lie. Do you hear me? You lie. What was the fight about?

ANN. Jack, don't stand there jammering and wasting time. You can settle that after.

HARWOOD. We got him, Captain.

RACKHAM. Who?

HARWOOD. The sea-artist. Hoy! Fetch him along, boys!

[*Men surge in with* EARLE.]

RACKHAM. Well, cock, we've got you. Red-handed,

[93]

as you may say.   You'll be red all over before we've done
with you.   Dumb, was you?   What've you got to say?
    EARLE.   Say?   What is there to say?   I'm paying a
debt.   That's what I'm doing.   A big debt to myself
and a bigger one to you.   You've killed all I had left
to live for and, thank God, you'll hang for it.   Now
do your worst.

[MARY *drops on side of* EARLE.]

    They told me you were dead.   I did it because I
thought you were dead.
    PIRATES.   Mucky story. . . . Tear the joints out of
him.   Up to the mast-head with him. . . . Fetch the
ropes, etc., etc.
    MARY.   Stand back. . . .
    EARLE.   I would have saved you.   You believe I
would have saved you?
    MARY.   Yes.   I believe you.
    EARLE.   Well, that's not such a bad end to a rough
voyage.
    RACKHAM.   You ain't had the end yet.

[EARLE *looks at him and turns again to* MARY.]

    EARLE.   Good-bye.   You have had a gift from me.
Give me a gift to take with me where I am going.
    MARY.   Yes, I owe you a gift, Ned.   And I'll give
you a gift and a good-bye.   It's the best I can do for
you, Ned.   (*She shoots him dead.*)
    SAILOR (*up on* P.S. *poop ladder*).   There's a frigate
rounding the Spit.   She's flying the Jack.
    FEATHERSTONE.   The Governor's ship.

[*Distant boom of gun heard.*]

    RACKHAM.   We're all dead men.
    MARY.   Mr. Featherstone.   All hands to fighting
stations.

[*Movement from all hands.*]

RACKHAM.   Belay there.   You're mad.   You can't fight him.

MARY.   We can't sink him, but we can fight him. Did you hear my order, Featherstone?

[*Another move from all.*]

RACKHAM.   Stand fast.   You can't take orders from Will Read.

VOICES.   Why not?

RACKHAM.   Will Read's a woman.

MARY.   What if I am a woman?   I've led the best of you before now.   You follow Ann Bonny and me, and we'll show you some sport before you die.   Man your guns.

[FEATHERSTONE *rings bell.* RACKHAM *falls on his knees praying aloud.*]

ANN (*to* RACKHAM).   Fight like a man if you don't want to die like a dog.

MARY.   There they go.   Get to your stations, cocks. Get to your prayers, Calico Jack.   I'll let you hear a woman having the last word.

[*All get to their stations.*]

That's the game.   Hoist the Black, Ann Bonny.

ANN (*running up* O.P. *ladder to poop*).   Aye, aye, Soldier.

MARY.   Wait till she rises with the sea.   Give me the linstock.   (*Gunner hands it to her.*)   Here's my message to Governor Rogers, the King of England, the whole world and God Almighty on his throne.

[*She fires the gun.*]

CURTAIN

[*After Curtain falls four shots are fired by the pirates and are answered by the Governor's ship.*]

ACT III

SCENE V

The scene opens in darkness. There is first a loud and insistent beat of waves through a mournful negro air which gradually grows.

As the noises die away the lights go up and show MARY READ *in bed in the prison lazaret at Port Royal in Jamaica. A red-nosed naval chaplain and a stout negress stand beside her bed. The time is the spring of* 1721.

CHAPLAIN.   Is she asleep?

NEGRESS.   I don't know, Master.   Sometimes I think she sleep and sometimes I think she dead.

CHAPLAIN.   Poor thing, poor thing!   The wages of sin.   The wages of sin in double measure.   It is a lesson to all of us.   A lesson to all of us. . . .

NEGRESS.   You like a-take 'nother little drop of rumbo to keep out the fever?

CHAPLAIN.   It might be wise.   It might be wise. Thank you, Aunt Cleopatra.

[*They drink.*]

MARY.   Who's that?   Is that you, Dick Corner?

CHAPLAIN.   Was that the man?   The—ahem— father of her child?

NEGRESS.   No.   No, Sah, no.   She never speak of him.   Right doggone unnatural that, come to think of it.

MARY.   Aunt Cleo.

NEGRESS.   What is it, my lamb?

MARY.   Where is my baby?

NEGRESS.   She done ask for de chile. . . . Never mind about dat, honey.   Never mind about dat.

[96]

CHAPLAIN (*affected and taking another dram*). Dear, dear! Oh, dear me!

MARY. No. I remember. He's dead too.

CHAPLAIN. The wages of sin is death.

MARY. What's that you said?

NEGRESS. Never you mind, honey, you go asleep once moah.

MARY. Is that the Chaplain?

CHAPLAIN. Yes, Mary Read. I'm here.

MARY. You are very good to be here. Why are you here?

CHAPLAIN. I am here, my child, to try to awaken in you a sense of sin. For without a sense of sin (here, put this glass down) there can be no repentance, and without repentance there can be no salvation.

MARY. You will have your work cut out with me. . . . And Jack Rackham. Where is Jack Rackham?

CHAPLAIN. Oh, dear. You must remember he was hanged six or seven months ago; as you yourself would have been but for the merciful and inscrutable intervention of . . oh, damn this business! See here, my girl, I am here to give you the consolations of religion, and the sooner you get into a proper frame of mind the better for both of us.

MARY. What is the proper frame of mind?

CHAPLAIN. Ain't you sorry for the life you've led?

MARY. No. (*Closes her eyes as if dying.*)

CHAPLAIN. Quick, quick, my Prayer Book. It's over there by the bottle. It's nearly all over now.

MARY (*very faintly*). No, I'm not sorry. I've led a gallant life. I've killed men, but always in fair fight and I've shown mercy to my prisoners. I've never robbed the poor nor wheedled the rich. I've never sold my soul for money or ease. I've never turned my back upon friend or foe. I've no woman's tricks, but I've no alderman's tricks either. I've never let cowardice stop me from doing anything under God's heaven. And I'll

[97]

not go out of this life cringing to you nor to any man.

CHAPLAIN. Mary Read, Mary Read, you can't go into the presence of your Maker with a story like that.

MARY. If my Maker doesn't like my story, He should have taken more pains when He made me. . . . But I think He *will* like it. (*She sinks back.*)

[*A trumpet is heard—faintly.*]

CURTAIN ON LAST NOTE.